the book of self-care

the book of self-care

Remedies for Healing Mind, Body, and Soul

mary beth janssen

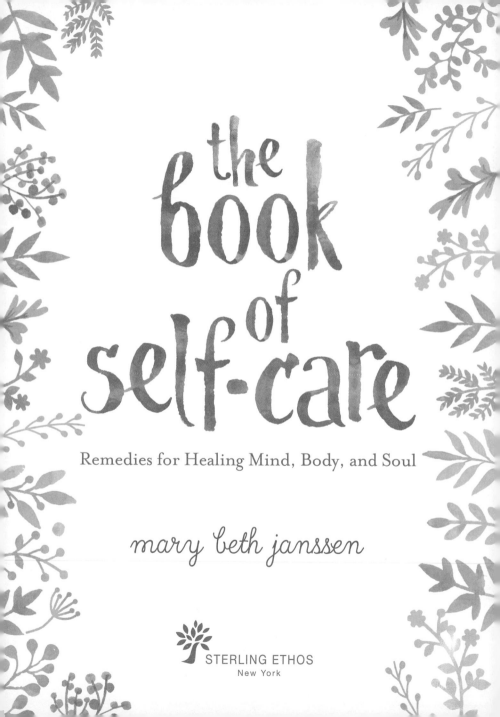

STERLING ETHOS
New York

This book is dedicated to my parents, Petronella and Hubertus,
and my life partner, James.
"You dance secretly inside my heart, where no one else can see."—Rumi

STERLING ETHOS
New York

An Imprint of Sterling Publishing Co., Inc.
1166 Avenue of the Americas
New York, NY 10036

ISBN 978-1-4549-2631-3

Distributed in Canada by Sterling Publishing Co., Inc.
Canadian Manda Group, 664 Annette Street
Toronto, Ontario, Canada M6S 2C8
Distributed in the United Kingdom by GMC Distribution Services
Castle Place, 166 High Street, Lewes, East Sussex, England BN7 1XU
Distributed in Australia by NewSouth Books
45 Beach Street, Coogee, NSW 2034, Australia

For information about custom editions, special sales, and premium
and corporate purchases, please contact Sterling Special Sales at 800-805-5489
or specialsales@sterlingpublishing.com.

Manufactured in China

10 9 8 7 6 5 4 3 2 1

sterlingpublishing.com

Design by Shannon Nicole Plunkett

contents

introduction

self-care: the ultimate health care

Complete health and awakening are really the same.

—TIBETAN LAMA TARTHANG TULKU

Tarthang's potent premise is at the Heart of true Self-care. No matter what your age, gender, ethnicity, or health profile, when you open your heart and awaken to who you really are—a spiritual being—your evolution, or *unfoldment* of your full human potential, begins. Not before.

When we intrinsically know that our awakened self is our eternal self, our true devotion to self-care—and thus a vital, fulfilled life—truly begins. Everything else is window dressing. Everything else is a distraction, or aversion to the truth. No amount of massages, hot baths, aromatherapy, healthy food, or exercise will sustain us over the span of our lives if not experienced from the layer of our being that is pure consciousness or spirit. Certainly they're part of self-care—and a very enjoyable part at that! After all, a popular definition of self-care is: the practices we engage

in on a regular basis to manage stress and enhance our well-being. However, chances are that unless performed from a place of exquisite mindfulness, our best self-care efforts may be a passing fancy, or be stunted or fall by the wayside, just like so many dashed New Year's resolutions. Oscar Wilde said it best: "To love oneself is the beginning of a lifelong romance." And if I may add, true, unabashed self-care is a lifelong romance with yourself. Self-love = self-care.

Becoming a Spiritual Warrior

So now take a moment and ask yourself: In this hyperkinetic, attention deficit, precariously stressful world that we live in today, how do you connect with your center—that inner place that enables you to practice extreme self-care—and make the most insightful, life-affirming choices? Being fiercely awake has never been more necessary for our transformation to sustainable, enduring, higher-vibrational levels of life balance and well-being. Every time we compassionately and consciously care for ourselves, our authentic self becomes more empowered, while our fearful mind (read: ego) grows weaker. Every self-care act we engage in is a powerful affirmation: *I honor myself and who I am becoming. I'm on my side. I've got this.* Repeat this affirmation to yourself right now.

Achieving Optimal Well-Being

Self-care is the ultimate healing mechanism for wholeness in mind, body, and soul. True health and well-being is much more than simply the absence of disease, injury, or infirmity, but rather it's a state of wholeness between mind, body, spirit, and environment: our extended body. In this state, the layers of our being are deliciously intertwined and in harmony with each other instead of engaged in a standoff. With the consciousness-based system of healing we'll share here, we commit to taking full responsibility for our health and well-being. This is preventative health care at its best.

This is "good medicine" and the best health insurance possible—to tap into our own incredible and innate healing capacity. We often turn our healing power over to others. It's important to see our physician(s) where warranted, but you have the ability to discern and intuit what will make your heart sing and balance your mind-body physiology. We simply need to tune in. Self-care is setting an inner tone in our heart, the seat of our soul. It is moving from our head to our heart. This is where our mindfulness is paramount. Then true self-care becomes a noun instead of a verb. "I AM self-care." Every choice we make can become the most life-affirming one possible, and be for our greater good. Will we screw up and backslide? Of course we will! We're human, after all. Send yourself loving-kindness, compassion, and forgiveness, and then continue on. But as we become more mindful in each moment of our lives and *train the mind to serve the heart*, an energetic shift takes place. And we may then indeed have the power within us to short-circuit any number of missteps, including the progression of disease. Many medical studies have indicated that mindfulness can positively affect physical health. I have witnessed this phenomenon again and again in the clinical work that I do. Remember: every choice we make can be good medicine—or poison. This book is an instructional manual of sorts that will help you learn to feel the difference between the two, tap into your own innate healing capacity, *and* become an intuitive healer—of self.

Yes, *self-care can save your life*. No, it will not spare you from your ultimate demise. However, when based in consciousness and practiced regularly, its healing capacity will diffuse stress; create peace, joy, and balance; prevent debilitating conditions; and, over time, can slow the potential onset of chronic *dis*-ease that can be energy draining and life altering. When my son William left his body, I set out on a path from which there was no turning back. Not to sound clichéd, but I began searching for the deeper meaning to life. I had been on the proverbial fast track to success as defined by society—but what kind of success was I as a human being? My ambitions and my attention were in large part externally focused. I was not following my own internal GPS, that's for certain. Regular self-care often fell low on the priority list because there were just so many other damn things that had to be done first to chase the cultural/societal dream of do more, have more, be more. So I learned how to meditate. And committed to it. I learned to drop into and open my heart. I became more and more mindful every day. I began asking the deeper questions. *Who am I? Why am I here? What is my purpose—my dharma.* It was kind of like jumping out of the frying pan into the fire, and then facing the results of this self-inquiry. But I knew there was no turning back. I now knew the truth. I felt as if my old self was slipping away. And, as it turns out, it was! And with this level of awareness, this level of mindfulness that meditation engenders in us, our old self will keep slipping away. Change becomes our friend. As Joan Didion so eloquently expressed, "I have already lost touch with a couple of people I used to be."

Every one of us will have these moments of truth in our lives that beckon us to wake up. Life-altering illness, loss and grief, and, yes, even anger—whether personal or planetary—crack our hearts wide open and serve as powerful catalysts to wake us up. They beg us to shake up the status quo. And once you've woken up, there is no falling back to sleep. With a heightened consciousness, I began to come face-to-face with my true nature—and the true nature of everything else. This was like the most sublime home-coming. Ultimately, as we awaken, every one of us wants to feel that there is some deeper meaning to our existence. From this place, we question our values, perceptions, and beliefs. That is where the real work of self-care begins. By nourishing ourselves, we are more able to see where we're blocking our abundance through our misconceptions and outdated, erroneous thought patterns. We also begin to see when our heart chakra instead of our root chakra is unclear and blocked by our undigested emotional mate-rial, which calls upon us to calm and clarify our spirits through heart-opening practices.

Join the Consciousness Revolution

Expanding our consciousness is one of the riskiest endeavors on earth. It endangers the status quo and disturbs our comfort zone. It calls upon us to make our lives congruent with our conscious-ness—to give as much attention to our souls as to the grooming of our bodies. It asks us to give as much attention to opening our hearts as to our calendars.

Self-imposed expectations of how life should be or could be can cause us great suffering. We tell blooming, expansion, development, unfolding into the best version of ourselves, into the spiritual beings that we are. Our devoted self-care regimen can remind us of this in every moment if we're engaged on the level of spirit. In the contemplative and mindful moments, we can reconnect with this knowledge over and over again.

There's no going back on this journey. What will be the spark that ignites this transformation, this metamorphosis from cocoon into butterfly? It will be an embracing of our wholeness, and giving ourselves the most heart-full, loving, compassionate, and consciousness-based self-care that we have to give.

On a Purely Practical Level

We're up to our eyeballs in all forms of stress management and wellness solutions today. Everywhere we turn, we're bombarded by messages, headlines, videos, books, classes, and more, all promising easy steps for managing stress and getting healthy, yet the daunting statistics show that the world's population is facing more health challenges than ever before. *Stress is at the root of chronic disease and is a killer.* Chronic diseases are the number one cause of death and disability in the United States, responsible for seven of ten deaths. Eighty percent of the over two trillion health dollars spent every year go to treating chronic illness. Chronic diseases include heart disease, stroke, cancer, diabetes, asthma, arthritis, and obesity, among others, many in large part preventable by modifying the risk factors. This begs the question, why are so many plagued by chronic disease in America and around the world?

Stress affects each individual differently. Some people are able to report the news from inside a hurricane; others are taxed by snarled traffic on their daily commute. Family, career, and life demands press in from all sides. As you rush to pick up the kids, your phone sends out a calendar alert to be across town for a meeting. Your head is elsewhere and you forget to pick up the dry cleaning. A boss demands a report while you are on the plane to the other side of the world for an important meeting. You arrive, stay up most of the night writing a great report for the boss, but blow the meeting. You know this is not the right way to live; you can feel it in your bones. We all know it: The World Health Organization has stated that between the early 1980s and 2009, stress rose 10 to 30 percent in all demographics all across America. As the information age dawned and grew, so did the stress levels of a nation.

With all this information coming toward us, why haven't we done better at coping with stress? Once called "exhaustion" or a "case of the nerves," stress's effect on the human body (and that includes the brain) was not known. Today we know differently. Most roads lead back to stress. Stress and its fall out—poor eating habits, sleeplessness, emotional upsets such as anger and mood swings, and much more—creates a vicious circle of stress, poor lifestyle habits, and, finally, internal inflammation that turns to pernicious disease.

Is it that we are overwhelmed by the plethora of information available to us, especially when it comes to choices we can make to better our lives? With an iCloud full of health information cir-cling the Earth, it is difficult to make sense of it all; you need a doctor at your side to riffle through it. But even that does not get you very far because you are specifically and wonderfully you. You are unique and you need to approach your health based on how your mind and body feel to you.

Certainly, we can do better than allopathic medicine's one-size-fits-all approach to treating chronic stress and ultimately, disease. If we become more conscious, awake, aware, and present, perhaps we can be more tuned in to how our lifestyle choices plant the seeds of illness. We can *feel* our health—or lack of it—through our attention.

You'd think that with traditional medicine's understanding of our bodies and the causes of disease along with the amazing tech-nological advancements of our time, we wouldn't be facing such daunting health challenges. But there appears to be a huge dis-connect between what we think, know, feel, and do that greatly impacts our well-being. There is a better way.

A consciousness-based system of healing will effectively close the gaps that exist between what we *do* and what we *know*, allowing us to mindfully make the most life-affirming choices for creating optimal health and well-being for ourselves. *This is about taking per-sonal responsibility for our own well-being and practicing preventative health care.*

Our committed, conscious, compassionate care of self is a brilliant adjunct to allopathic medicine. When followed, it may allow us to scale back on the more deleterious effects of "modern" medicine's protocols. By tapping into our own innate and unique healing capacity, we place ourselves in control over our own health and well-being. Rather than, "Doctor, fix me," the narrative now revolves around, "Patient, heal thyself."

Although our technologically proficient medical system has long been best at treating acute, not chronic, conditions, thankfully today's medical paradigm has invoked "person or patient-centered care" as a mantra. Bottom line? Compassionate self-care enables us to take responsibility and mindfully choose what kind of "modern" medical care to take advantage of as needed.

The consciousness-based, mind-body wellness approach to healing that is now fortunately beginning to take hold in the medical sector is the paradigm shift that our broken health care system needs. It's not about throwing the baby out with the bathwater when it comes to health care, but rather adding or integrating extreme self-care into your daily life as an important accompaniment to the more conventional allopathic approach to health care.

Why "Old School" Rules

Many of the "remedies" I'll be sharing here come from the wisdom traditions of yoga and Ayurveda and have been around for centuries. Yet, these traditions and their mind-body approaches to managing stress and creating balance have now been definitively proven through science and continual research studies to exert powerful healing results across a broad spectrum of health concerns. Many studies suggest that these healing systems/therapies may reduce cardiovascular disease risk factors, as well as prevent or treat certain cancers, infectious diseases, immune system deficiencies, hormonal problems, neurological disorders, mental health issues, addictions, and much more.

These natural systems of healing draw on elements of meditation (a primary preventative health remedy in Ayurveda and yoga), yoga asanas (postures), pranayama (healing breathwork), energy work, and nutritional wisdom, along with sensory modulation techniques including massage, aroma, color, and sound/music therapies. These wellness systems have emerged in an ever-growing number of hospitals, clinics, wellness centers, academic centers, yoga studios, spas, and even oncology wards. (I personally teach them in a number of these settings.) Their ability to gently, holistically heal make them the remedies of choice for true wellness seekers.

The bottom line, and the underlying message here, is to start with *you*. Understand the incredible healing capacity you have within. Seeking outside of ourselves for answers to our biggest challenges—disease management and prevention, emotional intelligence, relationships, self-esteem, addictions—can often lead us to feeling powerless and stuck. We can only change this by embracing that our ability to look radiant, feel energized, choose powerfully, and connect authentically and passionately with the world starts with a willingness to know, love, and care for ourselves—devotedly, intimately, unconditionally.

The Best Place to Start

I'm calling upon you to make yourself a sacred, nonnegotiable priority. Fall in love with taking care of yourself: Mind. Body. Spirit. Put yourself back at the top of your to-do list. Show up.

Regularly. Practice. Consistently. And please remember this: Life is not always shiny and full of namastes. I get that. Your practice doesn't expect you to show up happy. Trust me, I've been there. It simply asks that you be present. It doesn't mind if you've got it together, or if you're a mess. You can arrive with a chaotic mind and a heavy heart. Just get there. Start. Practice. You'll get better and better. And remember, it's never too late to get well, be well, and stay well.

Now, let us begin.

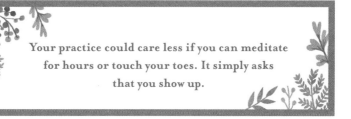

Your practice could care less if you can meditate for hours or touch your toes. It simply asks that you show up.

1

know thyself and
love thyself

*Weapons cannot hurt the spirit and fire can never burn him. Untouched is he
by drenching waters, untouched is he by parching winds. Beyond the power of sword
and fire, beyond the power of water and winds, the spirit is everlasting . . . never
changing . . . ever One. Know that he is, and cease from sorrow.*

—THE *BHAGAVAD GITA*

The ancient Oracle at Delphi said, "Know thyself." A perennial question on our spiritual journey is, Who am I? The essence of all knowledge is self-knowledge. But do you know who you really are? Though the basis of this quote is debated, some credit the Buddha as saying, "You yourself, as much as anybody in the entire universe, deserve your love and affection." Jesus told us to love our neighbors as ourselves. Both statements emphasize the idea that we shouldn't forget to love ourselves first. But how many of us really do? Affirm to yourself right here and right now: I am a citizen of the universe helping to raise the vibration of love here on earth, beginning with my self.

When we are intimately in touch with ourselves, we more readily afford ourselves the love and care that we so deserve. We make the fulfillment of our need for peace, happiness, and well-being a priority. Beyond basic physiological needs, fundamental human needs are for attention, affection, appreciation, and acceptance. These are all slightly different versions of the same thing: love. Whether giving to self, giving to others, or receiving from others, when we don't have these needs met, emotional discomfort, entropy, and ultimately *dis*-ease may ensue. So please, spill this love all over yourself and those you care for, and with a grateful heart, receive this healing energy from others.

The Real You

There is a beautiful ancient saying that I repeat often. This wisdom tells us to look at our body today to understand our past experiences and, if you want to know what your body will look like in the future, look to your experiences today. In navigating and creating wholeness in body, mind, and spirit—our spirit is the experiencer, our mind is where the process of our experience takes place, and our body is the end result of our experiences. So if you're not too happy with how your mind-body physiology is faring, you have the ability to change through your perceptions and experiences. Please don't bypass the experiencer or spirit, and get stuck only in the process—the layer of the mind where beliefs, untruths, misconceptions, and suffering can potentially and adversely affect our physical body. Rising above the chorus of emotion inside you is vital for well-being because we change the quality of our mind-body physiology by changing the quality of our experiences in consciousness. True self-care focuses on the mind-body connection, which teaches us that our experiences—including perceptions and lifestyle choices—are metabolized into molecules in our bodies. Every thought we have creates a molecule in the body.

These perceptions and experiences trip off a cascade of changes through the body's cellular community. As one of my mentors, Bruce Lipton, PhD, author of *The Biology of Belief*, writes: "The moment you change your perception is the moment you rewrite the chemistry of your body." Since our experiences are a result of our perceptions, if we change our perception we can change our experience (and therefore change our bodies). We change our perception through the expansion of consciousness in meditation.

Mind over Matter

As we engage, with full presence, in our self-care experiences, deep healing ensues—releasing a flood of feel-good chemicals into the bloodstream. This is now proven in *psychoneuroimmunology*—the science which studies the interaction between the mind and body and how this relationship affects blood chemistry and ultimately our well-being. We have the ability to change our neurochemistry. We have this natural pharmacy within us, including neurochemicals that help us heal—natural antidepressants, tranquilizers, painkillers, and growth hormone, along with immunomodulators, vasodilators—and so much more. Only one example of this mind-body connection is the effectiveness of positive affirmations, or good thoughts. It is scientifically proven that positive affirmations raise the immune system's white blood cell count. Amazing! Our well-being changes and evolves according to our experiences, but more importantly, our perception of those experiences.

Perhaps you've heard the saying "our issues are in our tissues," or "our biography is our biology." When we fail to feel and process our emotions, they sink into our tissues and make themselves at home there—only to unexpectedly and perhaps aggressively burst out at a later date, creating havoc. (See Chapter 9 on emotional cleansing.) Our mind and body are always communicating with each other, with our body listening in on our thoughts and reacting accordingly. Certainly this speaks to the mind-body connection. Simply stated, if we have happy thoughts, we create happy cells in our body; angry thoughts, angry cells; sad thoughts, sad cells—and so on.

Renowned neuroscientist Candace Pert, PhD, in her landmark book, *Molecules of Emotion*, wrote about the fact that every thought we have becomes a molecule in our body. Together with Solomon Snyder of Johns Hopkins University, Dr. Pert discovered endorphins, which are mood-enhancing, pain-reducing neurohormones. The word *endorphin* is short for "endogenous morphine," i.e., built-in heroin! It is released when we breathe deeply, exercise, receive a massage, make love, eat certain foods, and a whole host of other pleasurable self-care activities. The full benefit of the healing can only be experienced when we are fully present during these experiences. This will be our theme throughout this book: awakening to our wholeness, our divinity, to who we really are, through the exquisite self-care that we imbibe in and enjoy with our full attention.

You Are Pure Vibrating Energy

As experiences in consciousness go, all of creation is changing in every moment, including the human body. The human body is not simply static matter, but rather pure vibrating energy. A quantum physicist will tell you that if we go to the deepest level of our being, we are subatomic particles whirling around at lightning speed through vast open space, on the verge of becoming matter. And so, too, matter is always on the verge of becoming energy. This takes place through our energy or chakra system—the spinning vortices of energy aligned with our nerve plexuses along our spine.

Life's Cosmic Dance

This fluctuation of energy and matter is life's cosmic dance. Seven million red blood cells blink in and out of existence in your body every second. You shed 100,000 skin cells every minute! On a molecular level, your pancreas regenerates every twenty-four hours, your stomach lining every three days, your white blood cells every ten days, your brain protein every month, your liver every six weeks. As you can see, your body is constantly regenerating and rejuvenating itself—metamorphosing. Your body will be different by the time you finish reading this page. To successfully perform this renewal process, the human body needs simple, ongoing, and life-affirming nourishment in the form of optimal thought, food, and activity.

So coming full circle, if we sense that changing our experiences would benefit our mind-body physiology, we should do it!

Mindfulness can help us get there. Each person has the power to make choices that create balance and harmony in his or her life. The good news is that changing our experiences sometimes means little more than changing our perception of those experiences. When we regularly connect to the field of pure consciousness, or spirit, we begin the transformation.

Our Truest Self

"Out beyond ideas of right doing and wrong doing, there is a field. I'll meet you there."

—Rumi

Our spirit is floating fluidly and freely along the waves of another frequency domain—another energy "field." This is the field of pure consciousness, of infinite possibilities, of our pure potentiality. Spirit is spaceless, timeless, ageless, limitless, fearless. Spirit is infinite and eternal—this is the real you. Just as a Beethoven symphony is broadcast through a radio in sound waves, your central nervous system captures the real you—spirit—in your mind-body physiology. It gives your soul individualized form and broadcasts it throughout your body so you may experience your humanity within this existence. Just as Beethoven is not in the radio, the real you is not in your mind or your body. They are the earthly vessel for spirit. Depending on your level of consciousness, you will know this.

We are Multi-Dimensional Beings: Wholeness in Body, Mind, and Spirit

So to review, my friends: Our life consists of three layers of experience—body, mind, and spirit—or the experienced, the process of experiencing, the experiencer. Or the observed, the process of observation, and the observer. You get the idea. They're all different aspects of the same thing, the self. Remember, they are meant to be connected. Our inattentive mind creates any fragmentation between them.

The Body

The physical body is the *field of molecules* that comprise everything and includes our anatomical and energy bodies, as well as the environment or our extended body. These layers of our body are always in constant and dynamic exchange with each other. Every breath you take is a constant reminder of the conversation going on between your body and the environment. Our physical body is molecular "matter," and largely derived from the food we eat—underscoring the importance of maximizing our nourishment and minimizing toxicity wherever we can. Our energy body is comprised of vital energy or *prana*, which breathes life into bio-chemicals and orchestrates cells into forming the vibrant living beings that we are. (Our energy system also includes the 75,000 energy pathways called *nadis* circuiting through our body along with our chakra system, the Indian study of the seven spiritual centers in the human body.) Simply put, our body is always on the verge of becoming energy, and energy is always on the verge of becoming matter.

Our bodies are the most amazing instruments that we've been given in our time here. They're incredibly intelligent vessels—earthly vessels for spirit—yet many of us are so disconnected from the moment, even though we live in them our entire lives. Our bodies know what honors them. They pulse with evolutionary wisdom, yet we often zone out or anesthetize ourselves so that we fail to feel the constant signals of distress being sent our way. We try to commit to practices, programs, and strict routines in the name of self-care, but we end up compromising ourselves in the long run because we fail to take the first step in healing: we're just not listening. Every one of your sixty trillion cells is always speaking to you. The question is, are you tuned in and can you hear them?

"Nothing can pierce the soul as the uttermost sigh of the body."

—George Santayana

The Mind

The mind field (some might say minefield!) is where we experience emotions, feelings, and desires. Our intellect, a part of the mind, processes information, discriminates, and makes decisions. It's also where we experience ideas, concepts, and beliefs. These are what give rise to feelings, emotions, and desires. The ego is where we form our self-image and identify with the roles, positions, and possessions of our lives. The healthy ego, when in higher states of consciousness, ensures that our daily needs are being met so that we may fulfill our life's purpose. Conversely, when the puffed-up, overblown ego is in charge, it needs power, control, approval—all fear-based needs.

The Soul/Spirit

The field of pure consciousness, of our pure potentiality, of infinite possibilities is the deepest layer of our existence. It includes our personal soul; individual expression and spirit; all a universal expression of the field of pure consciousness. Our soul is conditioned by our past actions, or *karma*, which have planted seeds of unique memories and desires within our soul. Karma, memories, and desires could be called the *operational software* of our soul. They can guide us to the fulfillment of our soul's higher purpose. The universal layer of spirit is spaceless, timeless, ageless, and limitless. It, in turn, is the operational software for the entire universe, the "cloud" where we store everything.

Most of us will not fully dwell in this experience of pure consciousness. We dabble in it. We touch upon it in a limited manner when we temporarily suspend our thoughts through contemplative practice. Deep feelings of love, compassion, joy, peace, and creativity are but only some of the many ways we touch pure consciousness. In these moments of peak awareness, when we're wholeheartedly attentive, we forget who we are, what we want, and what our opinions are. We let go of all our baggage of mental and emotional constructs and we are fully present to our source, our essence, spirit.

Consciousness Is All

And speaking of consciousness: It is the essence of our being, the context of our lives. It is the source of the physical world. Consciousness is life itself. We are not doing consciousness.

Consciousness is doing *us*. And as one of my mentors Deepak Chopra states, "This is exactly what scientists are beginning to see. Scientists are beginning to see that it is not thoughts that are a product of molecules, but in fact molecules are structured out of fluctuations of information in a field of infinite information. That it is consciousness which is the phenomenon and matter which is the epi-phenomenon. It is consciousness which conceives, governs, constructs and actually becomes physical matter."

This includes our body. As we awaken to the spaceless, time-less, ageless, limitless, and fearless part of our being that is pure consciousness or spirit, our experiences are punctuated by peace, joy, passion, a need to care for and serve self and others, unity with all of creation, and a deep sense that love and compassion are at the center of everything. Self-care and, more broadly, self-love, self-growth, and self-creation are inextricably linked to our consciousness. Our regular connection to that layer of our being that is pure consciousness has the power to help us see and under-stand what we must do to heal and save ourselves from entropy and harm. From this place, we may steadfastly enact sustainable, life-affirming changes that allow us to go the distance.

Our consciousness, and its awakening, is the Holy Grail in enacting transformation of any kind. Any transformative technol-ogy, remedy, practice, or ritual trains our attention toward mani-festing true wholeness in mind, body, spirit, *and* environment. As we devote ourselves to this path of training our awareness, honing our concentration, heightening our consciousness to the choices we make, we do awaken. We deeply realize that we may have been betraying a harmonious inner universe by our choices, behaviors, attitudes, and beliefs. Whereas the disturbed, distracted mind has held us hostage until this point, we now wake up to the truth. As this realm of exquisite order, intelligence, and creative potential reveals itself to us, the veil lifts on those dissonant areas of our lives that beckon our attention. One can say that extreme self-care and radical self-acceptance become the matrix of true health and well-being.

States of Consciousness: Great Aspirations

There is a beautiful, short saying from the Greek Stoic philosopher Epictetus: "No man is free who is not a master of himself." All those centuries ago, he knew that the ultimate relief from life's pain and suffering came through an understanding of yourself and how you interact—and react to—the world.

We all have the power to raise our state of consciousness from ordinary waking, sleeping, and dreaming states until we reach the level where we get a "glimpse of our soul." Regular meditation gets us there. As we continue along the spiritual path to where we have such awareness, we move yet into a further heightened state of consciousness. We begin to understand and recognize that in all of our experiences, the spirit that is within us is also within everything that we perceive. When we fully awaken, we merge with spirit, and the whole universe becomes our body. The Vedas state, "As is the atom, so is the universe; as is the microcosm, so is the macrocosm; as is the human body, so is the cosmic body; as is the human mind, so is the cosmic mind." It is at this level of consciousness that we may realize who we truly are—self, spirit, the source and essence of creation. With this basic understanding, let's look at these levels of consciousness more deeply, shall we?

The Seven Levels of Consciousness

Many of us know quite well what the first three levels of consciousness are—waking, deep sleep, and dreaming—as interpreted by the layer of our mind. This includes our thoughts, emotions, memories, fears, and desires, and any other personal reactions that surface from our interaction with the external world. The majority of us spend most of our time in these layers of being. It is during meditation where we enter into a fourth level of consciousness. Speaking from the perspective of a yogi, in Sanskrit this is called *Atman Darshan*, meaning "a glimpse of the soul." It is the state of being in which we go into a deep inner silence—the gap between our thoughts—and commune with the core of our being, our inner essence. The longer you practice meditation, the closer you come to entering into a fifth level of consciousness called *cosmic consciousness*, where we have an awareness of spirit in the midst of every experience.

Turn your awareness to the one who is listening, who is observing, who is experiencing—right here, and right now. Do you feel the presence? This presence has always been there and always will be. This is the timeless factor in the midst of time-bound experience. Spaceless, timeless: this is the real you. The next level of consciousness is called *divinity consciousness*. This is where we have the experience of our divine nature in all the objects of our perception. This is where we understand that what is animating us is animating everything else in existence. We become intimate with the same spirit everywhere we go. And in the seventh level of consciousness, *unity consciousness*, we merge with it. The whole universe becomes our body. There is no longer any fear—especially of our mortality. There is only love. This is ultimate bliss.

Making the Connection

How do we connect with spirit? The following are a variety of practices that can bring exquisite mindfulness of the life-force energy that permeates and surrounds all of creation, propelling you into the field of pure consciousness, of infinite possibilities and your pure potentiality. We'll be exploring a number of them together throughout this book.

- **Become as mindful as possible, witnessing everything that you do.** Observe yourself reading this sentence right now. Who is the one reading? Be here now. When you shower, really feel the water on your skin. When you eat, really taste your food. When you're with someone, really be with him. Look into his eyes and see the soul that resides there. When you crawl into bed tonight, rise up above your body and observe yourself shifting from wakefulness to sleep.

- **Commit to the power of meditation, breathing exercises, positive affirmations, creative visualization, and physical activity such as yoga, Pilates, tai chi, or dance.** Seek out or create a labyrinth in your locale. Each practice serves to hone our sensitivity to mindfulness, allowing our spirit to soar into the realm of infinite possibilities.

- **Get lost in organic and sacred rituals.** Burn your favorite incense or candle, then connect with the aroma, the color, and the movement of the embers or flame. Play enchanting music, and then hear each individual note as well as the harmony. Read your favorite poetry aloud and listen to the rhyme and texture of the words.

- **Walk in nature.** Enjoy the sensual feast inherent in everything. Breathe from the prana-rich vegetation. See the smallest details in the clouds, trees, rocks, and water. See the universe in a leaf. See the divinity in a blade of grass, the petals of a flower. Feel the sun on your face, and the wind in your hair. Listen to nature's primordial sounds. Look for the man in the moon. If you can't go into nature in real time, visualize yourself there.

- **Make something beautiful.** Expand your creativity in new ways. Sketch, paint, mold clay, make a mosaic or an ornament. Coloring books have now become de rigueur for adults and can be meditative and relaxing. Cook colorful nourishing whole foods. Bake a cake. Get lost in the process, the doing whatever you decide to do. Whatever it is that you create exemplifies soulful organic beauty, do it, slowly and deliberately.

- **Create a vision or dream board.** Assemble a collage of images, pictures, and affirmations that express intentions, dreams, and things that make your heart sing. Creating a vision board can be a useful tool to help you define what your dharma is and what your goals are, and can serve as a source of motivation as you work toward manifesting your dreams.

- **Construct a small altar anywhere.** Some hang from the rearview mirror, some sit atop cubicles in the office. Small objects remind us of people and experiences and you can draw on the good feelings all day long. At home, altars can be more personal and include generations of family, beloved animals, important teachers and essential friends. It's all up to you. Every time you see the altar, you will be gently reminded of spirit's presence, eliciting tranquility and centeredness. Look to it especially when agitated or stressed. Breathe deeply until your center returns.

- **Write with your soul. Write. Keep a journal every day.** Write down whatever is on your mind, without editing or censoring. This is tremendously cathartic for your soul, allowing you to vent your feelings and see the areas in your life that need your attention. Do acknowledge good feelings, as well. This allows you to see and feel the grace surrounding you, and so you become an expression of this love and grace. No one will ever read this journal: It is yours alone.

- **Volunteer. Have empathy. Reach out and offer your services.** Ask, "How may I serve?" instead of "What's in it for me?" The great part is, when you give, you receive and science has proven it boosts your immune system. Taking time to reach out and help others is the best kind of remedy for your soul. Working on behalf of the good of another gets you out of the way. You can rise above your stressors and focus elsewhere. Volunteering has always been a way to contribute to the greater good and bring forth and lift your own spirit in the process. No matter where we are in life, we can contribute to make somebody else's day—and possibly life—better.

- **Cultivate peace in a garden.** This can involve a plot out back, a terra cotta pot on your veranda, and even working in a community garden. Visualize what your garden will look like after it receives loving care, and then set out to bring this beauty home. Tend it with your senses. Feel the dirt and pay attention to smell. In fact, you can plant scented plants and flowers that please you especially—calming lavender, invigorating rosemary, the soft licorice flavor of basil. Get "deep in the green" as the saying goes and find Earth. See your garden as a metaphor for your *inner* garden: planting, feeding, weeding, and harvesting. Then enjoy the harvest with joyful presence. Bring the outdoors inside as well with a lavender sachet or potted herbs on a windowsill.

- **Know that you are beauty personified.** Spend a day on yourself, indulging in beautifying rituals. Give yourself a full body massage with your favorite organic body lotion. Send yourself healing, loving energy as you nurture yourself in this way. Visit an organic spa. Let a cadre of beauty and wellness professionals nurture you and treat you to an experience of sheer bliss. Along similar lines, you might invite a friend over and perform soothing rituals for each other. Taking care of each other in this way is a healing, restorative moment for the spirit. We all crave the human touch.

- **Tune in to the cosmic rhythms of the universe—the calendar of the soul.** Just because we live by artificial light does not mean you shouldn't honor the sun, the moon, the stars. Celebrate the seasons. Is it spring, with blossoms opening and a general resurgence of energy everywhere? See this as a metaphor for your mind-body physiology. Change the way you eat to incorporate the foods ripening and hitting the market. Spend as much time as possible out of doors. Build in as much time as possible in your schedule to run and play. Is it winter, when life returns deep into the earth for a season of deep introspection? That's another great metaphor to feast on. Do you see a fireplace and piles of books? Will you daydream your greatest dream, looking into the fire?

- **Honor every significant stage in your life, as well as momentous stages in your loved ones' lives.** This may mean something as seemingly small as cutting out one hour of television every night to meditate, but it also includes major events like giving birth, getting married, or losing a loved one. Honor them all! Plan a gathering or celebration for major events. Smaller events— dessert in mid-week for a great report card, an unexpected gift to a friend who achieved a personal goal, or any tiny surprise for smaller events and achievements all offer a moment to expand the spirit and share a victory, no matter how insignificant.

Monkey Mind, Monkey Heart

Emoting without grounding, dancing in its confusion. Often misinterpreted as a monkey mind, the monkey heart is reflected in unsettled, repetitive thinking. To calm and clarify it, one may benefit from heartfulness practices: emotional release, armor-busters, depth charges, heart openers.

2

karma cleanse with loving-kindness, compassion, and forgiveness

Karma is not something complicated or philosophical. Karma means watching your body, watching your mouth, and watching your mind. Trying to keep these three doors as pure as possible is the practice of karma.
—THUBTEN YESHE

So let's get down to the serious business of honoring and loving ourselves unconditionally, shall we? In life, we tend to be hardest on ourselves, feeding ourselves a regular diet of the *shoulda, coulda, woulda's*—mental chatter about regrets from our past. This feedback loop of negativity does not serve our higher good. When you understand the role of karma in turning these thoughts into physical symptoms of either health or illness, you can make a conscious decision to thrive by sending loving-kindness, compassion, and forgiveness to yourself first and foremost, then paying it forward by doing the same for the people around you. This positive energy you give to yourself and others boosts your immune system!

We all have our own idea about the nature of karma. For some, the word has a more fear-based connotation—it signifies the negative repercussions of our thoughts and actions: "What goes around comes around." "You reap what you sow." Fear-based karma is always being afraid of the big "gotcha" that may be waiting for us right around the corner.

Karma is a Sanskrit word that means action and denotes a cycle of cause and effect that takes place in our lives—pure and simple. Our past actions condition our soul, planting the seeds of memories, desires, and intentions. When love based, karma can guide us to the fulfillment of our soul's higher purpose. Love-based karma is a gift that brings you lessons for your soul's personal growth and will continue to bring these lessons back around until you have learned them. It may take a lifetime, or many lifetimes, but it is certainly a most worthy endeavor to pursue.

Fear-based karma, however, is always about judgment, and how consequences are doled out to you or others based on your actions, whether positive or negative. Past karma is what it is, and we can burn off negative karma from our past starting in this moment through our loving-kindness, compassion, and forgiveness toward self and others. Going forward, there will no doubt be karmic episodes in our lives that will not honor our higher good. We're all human, after all. As much as we try to do our best in any given situation, our "best" may cause pain or heartache to others and certainly self. Who hasn't regretted choices that may have been hurtful? However, as we mindfully and with full intention travel our committed spiritual journey, we will experience less frequent challenging or difficult karmic episodes.

If we're awake, we will know in our hearts what the soulful, life-affirming choice in any given moment is; however, momentarily lapses of reason will continue to be part of life. Know that you can always press the reset button. Starting today, you can consciously choose love-based karma for your highest good. Any experience, positive or negative, can teach us important lessons. We can choose to learn from our actions and how they impact not only ourselves but others. Whether we are the transgressor, or someone else has committed transgressions against us, in soulful self-care, we would never hope that the offending party gets their karmic due. Rather, we can reach into our hearts and send loving-kindness, compassion, and forgiveness to ourselves or the other person or parties. We need to own any shade we throw at others, as well as stop wishing bad karma onto those who've hurt us. That will only cycle back around to us.

As NFL great Don Driver said, "Don't get mad. Don't get even. Do better. Much better. Rise above. Become so engulfed in your own success that you forget it ever happened." You are in the process of becoming the best version of yourself that you can possibly be, and you will use any difficult situations to autocorrect and set yourself back on the divine course of self-love and self-empowerment. We can karmically cleanse afflictions, provocations, insults, and injuries to ourselves and others by practicing loving-kindness, compassion, forgiveness, acceptance, and gratitude in all we think, say, and do. And make amends where possible, even if only in your own mind. In every moment of every day, we can be cleansing our karma through present-moment awareness of our thoughts and actions. In your life, try some or all of the following:

- Send love and light toward everyone, no matter what they've done.

- Ask yourself what your motives are, no matter what's happening, and make certain they're coming from a place of loving-kindness. Commit to no hidden agendas or control dramas, both signs of a puffed-up ego.

- Have an attitude of gratitude for everything, both positive and negative. However, do put a damper on negativity wherever and whenever you can. Negativity creates angry energy that comes back to you—a karmic boomerang, if you will. Feel it and release it.

- Keep this in mind: a life filled with acceptance is a life free of unnecessary emotional suffering.

- Practice forgiveness. Although difficult, it is one of the most important practices for manifesting love-based karma. Forgiving yourself is as important as forgiving others. Guilt is toxic—reliving mistakes over and over. Love yourself. Forgive yourself. There is not one human being anywhere who has not made mistakes.

 Let's Practice

Have you ever wondered what would happen if you continuously viewed others as just an extension of you? (Which they are!) Every encounter, conversation, conflict, and loving bond is you, facing your own reflection. Would your actions change if you always accepted the "outside" as your internal mirror? Stop looking to environment and every aspect of your life will become an intimate introspection. Naturally, one must maintain divine delicate balance with this practice. It could be easy to "overdo" and take on things that are not ours, or misinterpret the length, width, and depth of reflection seen as expressed through self. Sometimes what we see in another exists in self on the most minuscule of levels or vice versa. Let your uber-consciousness guide you here.

....

Spirit Is Love

Our intention as spiritual beings having a human experience is to learn, manifest, heal, and love at the "soul level." This is true self-care. Fulfillment, growth, and well-being happen at this level of our being. Please recognize your power of love to heal because spirit *is* love. *The common denominator in all healing is love.* Healing is the application of loving to the places in us that hurt. The nature of the universe is love and our natural human state is love. Love *is* our core nature. We feel so good when we give and receive love because this is what spirit does! Spirit is not fearful. Spirit is not hurtful. Spirit has no agendas. Spirit doesn't engage in any control dramas. Spirit is pure unadulterated love.

When love (spirit)—the most powerful force in the universe—is applied to hurt, we heal, expand, and transform on all levels of our being: mentally, physically, emotionally, energetically. And when we miss this opportunity to heal through spirit, that's okay. Simply know that you'll continue to experience the same type of

The Law of Karma

I've been teaching Deepak Chopra's Seven Spiritual Laws of Success in my seminars and workshops for some time now. The Law of Karma is always of great interest to my students. Here it is in adapted form:

Every action generates a force of energy that returns to us in like kind. When our actions bring happiness and success to others, the fruit of our karma is happiness and success.

I'll practice the Law of Karma by making a commitment to the following:

* Today I'll consciously witness my choices in each moment. The best way to prepare for any moment in the future is to be fully conscious of my choices in the present.

* Whenever I make a choice, I'll ask myself: "What are the consequences of this choice I'm making?" and "Will this choice bring fulfillment and happiness to me and anyone else affected by this choice?"

* I'll then ask my heart for guidance and listen for its message to me. If the choice feels comfortable, I'll plunge ahead with abandon. If the choice feels uncomfortable, I'll pause and envision what the consequences of my action could be. This guidance will enable me to make the most life-affirming choices for myself and for all those around me.

"problems" over and over again until you learn the lessons being presented to you. Though the life experience often feels otherwise, these lessons are always positive and serve as catalysts for our growth and fulfillment to higher levels of consciousness or being. View any and all challenges in your life as blessings and notice how, as you overcome them, you grow spiritually.

The Heart of the Matter

Our heart chakra *is* the energetic center of loving-kindness and compassion. Positively affirm right now: I open my heart to a flowing reservoir of love and compassion. I am love and I am loved. I am delighted and joyful for the unfolding of others to their full human potential. I open my heart to embrace all of creation as my earthly family. As I willingly let go of the past, I forgive myself and others. I love unreservedly, unabashedly, unconditionally!

Western medicine has typically seen the heart as a pump, beating on average seventy-two times per minute, roughly 100,000 times per twenty-four-hour period. Our heart sends anywhere from five to twenty-five quarts of blood through 60,000 miles of blood vessels every minute and helps in circulating more than 100 million gallons in a lifetime.

And we're learning so much more every day. Neuroscience tells us how the heart begins beating in the fetus before the brain is fully formed—indicating that the heart *is* the beginning of life in physical form. It also has discovered over 40,000 nerve cells in the heart alone, indicating that it has its own independent nervous system, sometimes called *the heart brain* or *brain in the heart*. Our heart has an electromagnetic field 5,000 times greater than that of the brain, and our heartbeat frequencies can be measured up to ten feet beyond our physical body. Each heartbeat creates an electromagnetic wave that washes over every one of the sixty trillion cells in our body, and every single one of these cells—from the tips of our toes to the crown of our head—is being vibrated by our heart. With each heartbeat, all our hearts are literally talking to one another in electromagnetic pulses. We're immersed in each other's heartbeats. If you lovingly talk to your own heart, you'll "auto-magically" know how to talk to others, often without having to even say anything with your mouth or brain.

This validates spiritual teachings that our energy fields are constantly intermingling with each other, enabling healing (or toxic) thoughts to be in constant exchange with each other. This also explains the expression "good vibrations," as in good energy flowing outward. The heartbeat's electromagnetic field might also explain why we may sense bad vibes after only just entering a room. In the same way, this may be why some people can cheer us up or calm us down by just being present. Good energy may flow outward from and surround these persons and they may have mastered the ability to send these good vibrations out into the universe.

Since the heart's energy field is greater than the brain's, energy and information sent from the heart to the brain can have a profound effect on our brain function, heightening intuition, creativity, and feelings of well-being. It's now well-known that this state of harmony or coherence between the heart and the brain helps us manage stress, boost creativity, and manifest peace of mind!

There has now been a tremendous amount of medical research exploring the heart's ability to metabolize harmony, peace, and love. Studies indicate that we humans possess incredible healing capabilities when we learn to open our hearts. Studies at the Institute of HeartMath®—a world leader in technologies for synchronizing our hearts with our brains—asked people to focus on feelings of love and appreciation whenever they began to feel angry or frustrated. After one month of this practice, study participants levels of DHEA (Dehydroepiandrosterone), the antiaging hormone, had increased 100 percent. Their levels of the stress hormone cortisol decreased 23 percent. It was also found that 80 percent of these people experienced slowed breathing rates and their hearts became synchronized with their breathing. In control groups, there were no physical or hormonal changes. The researchers' conclusions have proven the tremendous implications for our health and well-being. With feelings of love, our inner systems synchronize. This affects our immune system, our hormones, our cognitive function, and so much more.

The Seat of the Soul

With this powerful coherence starting in our heart rhythms, many posit that the heart may be considered the conduit through which consciousness enters humans at birth. This scientifically validated heart coherence supports many spiritual teachings that our heart is the seat of our soul. This also speaks to humanity's ultimate and healing intention to join our coherent heart energies into one unified love-based consciousness. We can train our brains to become exquisitely mindful and supportive of the heart energy intentions of love. Our coherent hearts in concert with proper brain development help us to attain our purest expression of love and, ultimately, of knowing God.

Opening Your Heart

Follow this simple practice to shift your outward flow of loving energy, moving away from your fears and toward your affirmation of all that is positive and onward to your field of pure conscious-ness—that field of pure potentiality and infinite possibilities in your life.

Sit or lie down. Make sure you're comfortable. With eyes closed and breathing deeply, gently place your palms against your heart center in the middle of your chest. Bring all your attention to your heart center. Now, as you breathe, send lov-ing energy directly into the center of your chest. Gently and tenderly hold the breath here to a count of four. As you breathe out, sense your breath moving into your palms. Each time you breathe in and out, feel the love and warmth being exchanged between your heart center and your hands. With your attention and intention on this exchange, feel a sustained and expansive warmth and tenderness. Begin to slowly move your hands away from your chest, keeping your focus on the love-filled energy being transmitted between your heart and your hands. Stay with and intensify these feelings of warmth and love you feel within this space. Continue to slowly widen this space, keeping your focus on this powerful and expansive love-filled energy. Now, with your love-filled wingspan, imagine broadcasting these feelings outward to anyone you choose—including yourself, of course. Sending out this positive heart-filled love energy to others and to the whole of creation is balancing and raising your vibration. High vibration energy of this kind is one of the greatest healing mechanisms ever. For you, and everyone surrounding you. You are affecting the collective consciousness; you are affecting the Earth.

After trying this practice, there is a natural progression to this next one: Try hugging someone lightly (heart to heart, left side to left side) and tune into the energy between you. Gently and delicately, send this person your heart vibrations filled with love and warmth. This type of energy exchange can relax and revive you, and deepen your communion with others. It actually releases oxytocin, the love hormone, into both you and your heart-hug recipient's mind-body physiology.

Other practices for opening the heart include: breathing in your own or someone else's pain and breathing out love and peace. With each breath in, inhale the pain, then exhale love. You can also radiate your brilliant spiritual light. First, bathe in the beautiful radiant being of light that you are. Imagine a brilliant light in your heart center that is shining upon everyone and everything. If experiencing a conflict or difficulty with someone, consider this bright light as a sort of spotlight. Keep broadening the area upon which your spotlight shines, until finally it illuminates the truth behind the conflict. Look closely at the conflict, express gratitude for it, and explore what it has to teach you.

....

A Short Word About Breath

How can we not know how to breathe? you ask. It's an automatic function! But the reality is that many people spend a great deal of the day breathing too fast—fourteen to twenty breaths a minute, or three times faster than is optimal for human health. Since breath, mood and emotion are all closely linked, rapid shallow breathing actually increases stress or a kind of panicky "panting" feeling. Shallow rapid breathing triggers muscle tension, sweat production, heart rate, and blood pressure. So, learn to master your breath. Patricia Gerbarg, MD, assistant clinical professor of psychology at New York Medical College, says that 5–6 breaths a minute will help you feel your best.[*]

The anatomy of each breath is broken into three parts: belly, diaphragm, and chest. Pull in air with your belly—it will naturally rise—and let your lungs fill. This should feel like your abdomen is being scoured clean with air. Take a moment after your lungs are full to feel the energy the oxygen has brought to body and spirit. Slowly release—your stomach will naturally fall—until your lungs are empty. Pause. Repeat. Pay attention to your breath traveling up and down your being. Your goal is 4–6 deep satisfying breaths a minute. The effect centered, calming breath has on the spirit is profound, transformative, and essential for an aware, engaged spirit and a healthy, oxygenated body. Think of this as one of your sole needs, like water and food.

In chapter 8, we'll explore breath in depth. It deserves an entire chapter because it's that important.

[*]Brown, Richard MD and Gerbarg, Patricia MD, *The Healing Power of Breath*, Shambala, 2012.

Loving-Kindness Meditation

One of the best ways to open your heart and soul is the loving-kindness meditation, a technique taught through the ages as a balm for the soul. Developed from the Buddhist tradition and now used by everyone, this meditation reaches deep inside the soul and evokes feelings of love, compassion, peace, and acceptance of all things. It unleashes the power of unconditional love, one of the strongest forces on Earth. It heals wounded things.

If you practice love with intention, and truly use this energy on thought and deed, transformation is yours. Buddha taught us that the mind is naturally radiant and pure, and it is this radiance and purity you access when you practice loving-kindness. Anger, greed, gluttony, resentment, rumination, and depression are all manifestations of pain. The more you cultivate love, the more these difficult feelings subside and positive feeling rises. The vibration you put into the world as you love will come back to you in ever-increasing waves of peace and quiet joy.

When we put love first, we see rather than look. We include rather than exclude; we commune rather than chatter. We care rather than remain indifferent. The world needs this badly. When we put love first, we invoke the blessings of the word *Namaste*. The word means, "the spirit in me honors the spirit in you. We are all one." That is a short, powerful prayer. It's a beautiful word to say and hear. Say it yourself as you have moments of peace and exhilaration throughout your day, whether you are meditating or just finished your daily chores.

Let's do a Loving-kindness meditation:

1. Sit or lie down in a comfortable position, with your spine reasonably straight. Gently close your eyes. Bring attention to your heart chakra, emanating from the center of your chest. Breathe in and out through your heart center. Witness the inflow and outflow of the breath. Feel it. Track it as it moves into your lungs and up your chest. The heart, mind, and body will begin to soften and release any held stress.

2. Begin with loving-kindness thoughts directed toward yourself. If you sense blockages or negative feelings, imagine dropping beneath them to the place where your only desire is to care for yourself and be safe and well. Breathe deeply, slowly and consistently until your body calms, your thoughts slow. You can use phrases such as, *"May I be safe and protected from harm. May I be deeply joyful. May I be peacefully at ease. May I be healthy and strong." Or, make up your own. Use whatever thoughts strengthen and calm you. Express your hopes for yourself and your life.*

3. Gently repeat the phrases again and again, letting the feelings that arise move through your being. Do this for one minute, five minutes, or twenty minutes, whatever time allows. If your mind wanders off, don't worry. Gently witness your lapsed attention, and bring it back to focus on the loving-kindness phrases. Be there for yourself. Be in the moment with these positive statements, feeling their vibration resonate through your whole being.

4. Now think of someone in your life about whom you care deeply: a parent, spouse, dear friend, or teacher. Visualize this person and now direct loving-kindness their way: *"May you be safe, be joyful, be at ease, be healthy and strong."* Make up your own. Repeat the phrase again and again as time permits. You are a broadcaster of energy. Tune in to the broadcasting of these feelings, this energy. Feel them move out of you, traveling toward their recipient and once landing, transforming life. Give your feelings and thoughts wings.

5. Next, consider someone who is having a hard time in his or her life right now. Feel their presence. Now offer loving-kindness to this person: *"May you be safe, be joyful, be at ease, be healthy and strong."* *Say to them whatever loving words come to your mind. Providing support and strength to someone struggling is one of the deepest satisfactions you might experience. And paradoxically, the more strength you give out, the stronger you will grow. How many lives have been saved by a kind word or thought delivered at just the right moment?*

6. Now think of someone in your life who plays a more neutral role, whether it be a cashier at the grocery store, a bus driver, a clerk at the dry cleaner, or a gas station attendant. Imagine being with this person, and feel his or her presence. Now, offer loving-kindness to this person. *"May you be safe, be joyful, be at ease, be healthy and strong."* Every life you touch matters—for them and for you. This is how you grow your community, your sense of place in a large, sometimes seemingly indifferent world. It is never cold and uncaring if you are in it.

7. We've come this far. Now we're ready to expand our loving-kindness outward toward all of creation. Send out your boundless love without reservation: *"May all living beings be safe, be joyful, be at ease, be healthy and strong."* This unbounded loving energy can deeply heal and transform you, your friends, you acquaintances, your community, your region, your country, your planet. This loving-kindness is for the smallest bug in the lifecycle of a forest to the leaders of the G8. This is the great reach for the whole. Practice. Then practice again.

8. Gently come out of this meditation, taking this energy with you as you go about your daily activities. Use this practice anywhere: at the doctor's office, a business meeting, or home. If you practice it among others, you'll immediately feel a wonderful connection to whomever you meditate about. Deep love and affection will grow, along with healing benefits. Remember, when you give, you receive. When you share your powerful loving-kindness energy with self and others, you are boosting your immune system!

Have Compassion

"If your compassion does not include yourself, it is incomplete."
—Jack Kornfield

An important partner to loving-kindness is the practice of compassion.

With the high level stress that surrounds us, what can we do to bring peace and harmony into our lives? We can begin by having compassion for self and others—the ultimate sign of emotional maturity. I guarantee this richness will come around to reward you handsomely. Compassion as a practice is where we're able to have understanding, patience, and sympathy for distress—whether our own or someone else's. We learn to not be so hard on ourselves and others. It's so important to be kind, because we are all carrying a heavy burden. When we are compassionate, we are working on creating awareness within ourselves that we're all doing the very best that we can from the level of consciousness that we're in. When we try to understand where someone else is coming from—whether from a place of pain, hurt, anger, pride, low self-esteem—we automatically become less judgmental. And with this we become more tolerant. When we become more tolerant, we are more readily able to forgive. And with a forgiving heart, we may drop the burdens of anger, resentment, and sadness that contribute to our stress. When we learn how to walk in someone else's shoes, we find it easier to open our heart and love unconditionally.

The Science Behind Compassion

Compassion is neuroscience's latest frontier. Growing research shows compassion's effect on improved health, happiness, and longevity. Compassion meditation lessens "mind-wandering," galvanizes one's attention, and encourages benevolence toward self and others.* And the real clincher? A study by Jordan Grafman at the National Institutes of Health indicated that brain

*Clifton B. Parker, "Compassion meditation reduces 'mind-wandering,' Stanford research shows," Stanford News Service, April 22, 2015.

imaging shows how the practice of compassion stimulates the same pleasure centers associated with the desire for food, water, and sex. We can infer, then, that compassion is an essential—like food, water and sex.

"We are seeing a revolution in how the mind works. As little as two weeks of practicing compassion with intention has a positive physiological effect on the body. It can lower blood pressure, boost your immune response and increase your calmness," says James Doty, MD, professor of neurosurgery at Stanford University and founder of Stanford's world-renowned Center for Compassion and Altruism Research and Education (CCARE). CCARE is at the forefront of an emerging mental health movement that strives toward fewer pharmaceutical interventions and more emphasis on our innate natural healing traits such as empathy, altruism, kindness, and resilience. (Interestingly, Doty's center was set up with the largest donation ever made by the Dalai Lama to a non-Tibetan cause.)

Doty adds, "People are much happier and live a better life if they are able to maximize their genetic potential for being compassionate, and it has a significant contagion effect on others, motivating them to be more kind."

Borrowing from Buddhist traditions, compassion practice uses mindfulness techniques, meditation, visualization, and breathing to develop nonjudgmental awareness of our own as well as other's distress and pain. Not only does this calm the nervous system and boost feelings of contentment and self-worth, but it also fosters deep communion with others by focusing on our shared experiences rather than our differences.

Let's Practice

Let's put this into practice for a moment, shall we? Close your eyes, drop into your heart, and say to yourself, *"May I and the whole of creation be free from suffering and its causes."* Repeat this to yourself for a couple of minutes.

Brava! You've just experienced the vast, beautiful mind of universal compassion, often referred to as "Buddha mind." You have poured innumerable blessings into your being and into all sentient beings. Just imagine if we could practice this all the time, allowing our compassion to become as expansive and all encompassing as possible!

....

To Forgive Is Divine

"To err is human; to forgive, divine."
—**Alexander Pope**

"Holding onto anger is like drinking poison and expecting the other person to die."
—**Unknown**

Are you good at playing the blame game? Good at getting down on yourself? When wronged, do you hold on to anger, resentment, and grudges? Do you think about seeking revenge or getting even? If yes, it's important to realize that failure to forgive—whether yourself, or others—causes stress that is ultimately poisonous to your body, mind, and soul.

When we fixate on revenge, we become a victim who has turned our power over to someone or something else. As you hold on to these toxic thoughts, they affect you and your well-being—not the person that you feel offended you. Let go and let God, as the saying goes.

It is so important to not feel victimized. When you assume the role of the victim and fail to let go, your body continues recycling the same negative energy. You find yourself living in the past, unable to move forward, live in the moment, and experience joy. This affects your bodily systems—immune, metabolic, hormonal, cardiovascular, neurological, and more. And do keep in mind that if you forgive, it doesn't necessarily mean that you condone what happened. This is about catharsis, and preventing that negative energy from becoming locked up inside you. Forgiveness releases tension and stress, letting us feel at peace. This is about feeling strong and healthy. Mahatma Gandhi said it best: "Forgiveness is the attribute of the strong." Let's be strong and resilient beings, and have a forgiving heart. Our wholeness depends on it.

Steps to forgiveness:

- Give yourself some quiet time. Consider a grievance or punishing grudge against yourself, someone else, or an offending event that has taken place. Consider the details without becoming emotionally charged. Deep breathing can help with this. Stay as detached as possible, as if watching the event on a screen.

- Holding this image in your mind, have the intention to forgive, and release the hold—whether sadness, disapproval, or condemnation—that the offense has on you. Say out loud or to yourself: "I forgive myself/[the person who hurt you] for the pain/anger/bitterness that I/they caused."

- Visualize how exhilarating it will feel to no longer have this affliction haunting you and constricting your energy. Talk about taking a load off your shoulders—and your heart, along with hormonal, nervous, and immune systems—very freeing indeed!

- Kiss and make up with yourself or the person that you've hurt, or who has hurt you. Ask for or offer forgiveness. Yes, it's daunting. But keep in mind that you're coming from a place of peace, love, and understanding. Stand where your feet are and come from a place of inner strength. You may need to offer forgiveness energetically, if it cannot be done in person. And you may even send or ask for forgiveness from those who may have left this earthly plane. It still counts.

- Fortify your strength and resolve by asking for help from the depths of your soul, a higher power, nature, your fellow human beings, or whatever source you draw your power from.

- Tune in to every nuance of change in your thoughts, feelings, and relationships, with patience and awareness. Forgiveness encourages change and great healing to take place. Please do not rush this process. Bathe in it. You've created an energetic shift within yourself and your surrounding environment.

Do consider how you apologize. I'm a huge fan of replacing "I'm sorry" with "Thank you." Instead of saying, "I'm so sorry I'm late," say, "Thank you so much for waiting for me." Do you feel the shift in energy? Or, instead of saying, "I'm sorry for being such a mess," say, "Thank you for always loving and caring about me." You're not only feeding yourself this wonderful positivity, but as others receive your gratitude instead of your negativity, there is the potential for improving relationships.

In addition, take responsibility for your actions when you apologize and do not accept passive apologies that show the offending party does not take responsibility for their actions.

For instance, instead of saying, "I'm sorry this offended you," say, "I'm sorry I was offensive." Or, instead of saying, "It was just a joke," say, "Some things should not be joked about."

And do remember, forgiveness does not mean that you condone what happened or are saying that it's okay. It may never be okay. But by forgiving, you release the constriction of energy surrounding your being and your heart, as well as the person or event, and you are able to move onward. Instead of living in the past, you're joyfully free to live in the present.

Vitamin Forgiveness

To err is human, to forgive is smarter . . . at least this is what studies suggest. Growing evidence shows that those inclined to forgive enjoy better physical and mental health than those prone to grudges. In studies, adults were asked to use either forgiving or unforgiving imagery as they thought about someone who had wronged them. Those thinking "no mercy" experienced a significant rise in heart rate and blood pressure, while their moods worsened. Those who imagined showing forgiveness had healthier vital statistics, and who knows how much more peace of mind.

3

stress less

Health and disease don't just happen to us. They are active processes issuing from inner harmony or disharmony, profoundly affected by our states of consciousness, our ability or inability to flow with experience.

—MARILYN FERGUSON

This chapter is about how uncontrolled and toxic stress deeply affects our health. You'll have the tools to maintain your overall wellness when you fully understand the importance of consistent lifelong vigilance toward self-care and self-love.

The word *stress* evokes all kinds of unpleasant imagery: pain, anger, depression, exhaustion/sleeplessness, addictions from workaholism to alcoholism, as well as a number of other "isms." Our lifestyle determines so many of these stressors, including work-family conflicts, toxic relationships, financial pressures, and feeling as if there's never enough time. Research clearly shows that unmanaged, long-term chronic stress breaks us down mentally, physically, and emotionally. Chronic stress even harms our DNA! *Telomeres* are protective casings at the end of each strand of DNA. Each time a cell divides, it loses some of its telomeres. An enzyme called *telomerase* can replenish it, but chronic stress and exposure to cortisol, the hormone triggered by stress, decrease your supply over time. When the telomere is too diminished, the cell often dies or becomes inflamed. This greatly affects our health and longevity.

Stress is at the root of chronic disease and is a killer. As discussed earlier, chronic diseases are the number one cause of death and disability in the United States, responsible for seven of ten deaths. Chronic diseases include heart disease, stroke, cancer, diabetes, asthma, arthritis, and obesity, among others—with many in large part preventable by modifying risk factors. This begs the question, why are so many plagued by chronic disease in America? What prevents us from instituting health-optimizing changes into our lives that prevent or modify disease processes, and bolster a joyful, fulfilling, sustainable quality of life? I'll postulate that it's a lack of consciousness to these matters. We are not awake and without awareness, there can be no change.

War or Peace

When we're constantly in stress mode, we are slowly ruining our health. There is a better way. When we understand how stress can severely denigrate our mind-body health, we can commit with full awareness to transforming our relationship with it. It's in large part about perception. Remember what Bruce Lipton, PhD, taught us in a previous chapter: "The moment you change your perception, is the moment you rewrite the chemistry in your body." Research shows that those who believe their stress is a normal part of life actually have a reduced risk of stress-related illness or death.

Stressed Is Desserts Spelled Backward

A mentor of mine in the stress space, Brian Luke Seaward, PhD, had an epiphany that created a turning point for him from a childhood filled with incredible stress caused by his alcoholic parents. One day, his sweet grandmother handed him a plate of freshly baked cookies with the loving words, "Now, remember, stressed is just desserts spelled backwards!" He came to realize how humor and compassion could powerfully ease both stress and sorrow and has made it his life's work to remind people that, as he writes, "We have the power to move through, or around, our problems, and eventually transcend them." I highly recommend Brian's book, titled *Stressed Is Desserts Spelled Backwards* after his grandmother's encouraging words.

Stress or Balance?

We are the sum of what we think, feel, and do. These activities combined go into making up our mind-body health profile.

What starts as a response to pressure becomes a lifestyle. When we regularly indulge in stress-inducing behaviors, we are not honoring our wholeness, or, as American writer and mythologist Joseph Campbell says, "following our bliss." Disharmony sets in. If we consistently are on high speed, keep our life and activities on fast-forward, skipping meals or eating junk foods, smoking, taking drugs, forgoing exercise, sleeping poorly, lacking direction and focus, and perpetuating a pessimistic view of life without any kind of spiritual connection, we *are* placing ourselves at risk for catastrophic illness. At the very least, problems will become chronic if we don't wake up to the debilitating effects of unmanaged stress.

> **Seventy to ninety percent of doctor visits are attributable to stress—whether physical, mental, emotional, or environmental, according to the medical professionals at WebMD.**

Stress by definition is the inability to cope with a threat, real or imagined, to our well-being. This results in a series of responses and adaptations by our minds and bodies. We all respond differently to the perceived stressors coming our way. For example: You may respond to a traffic jam on your commute to work with anger and frustration. Someone else may view the situation as a time to relax and get away from it all, listening to soothing music. The latter response is borne of mindfulness strategies that can help you cope. By adjusting your perspective, you'll be able to focus on your feelings in the present moment and do what is necessary to calm your nervous system. (See the next chapter for more information on mindfulness strategies.)

Our ability to cope is crucial. After all, stress is a normal part of life, and the way in which we experience it can be positive up to a point. Called *eustress*, this positive type of stress makes our lives meaningful. It tells us how much we care about the people and activities in our lives. It helps us channel our energy to be strong, to be resilient, to perform at our best. In a balanced life, eustress is manageable and can give us uncommon strength and fortitude to face a challenge or a perceived threat.

Physiologically, all stress is triggered by the body's instinct to defend itself—the "fight or flight" response—which is useful for emergencies like defending yourself against an assailant, dashing out of the path of a speeding car, or fleeing a burning building. But stress that is allowed to hum along unabated in response to life's daily challenges becomes *dis*tress, responsible in turn for a wide ranging assortment of chronic and acute *dis*-ease.

Welcome to the HPA or hypothalamic–pituitary–adrenal axis (the endocrine/hormonal glands responsible for kicking our stress response into high gear). When stressed, our hypothalamus tells the pituitary gland to tell the adrenal glands to start pumping hormones into our bloodstream. Our bodies respond to stress by manufacturing the stress hormones adrenaline and cortisol along with other corticosteroids, which help us respond—to fight or take flight—as needed in extreme situations. But when we make too many of these hormones for a long period of time, they wear down our bodies and our minds. Constant fight-or-flight plants the seeds for potentially serious health problems. Here is just a short list of what uncontrolled stress can manifest:

- The heart beats faster and pumps more blood. There is measurable incoherence in the heart rhythms. Blood pressure rises. This can contribute to coronary heart disease, as well as atrial fibrillation.

- Increased stress hormones cause anxiety, insomnia, addictions. Excessive cortisol zaps brain function, affecting cognitive function and memory retention.

- The pancreas releases more glucagon and less insulin, raising blood sugar. This can cause diabetes and obesity.

- Blood is shunted away from the digestive organs to the muscles, resulting in gastrointestinal problems.

- The body releases less rejuvenating sex and growth hormones (especially DHEA), which can lead to infertility as well as premature aging from wrinkled dry skin to sparse hair.

- The immune system is suppressed, impacting the body's ability to fight infections.

- Blood platelets become stickier, building up in arteries, which can lead to heart attack and/or stroke.

- Wide-ranging problems affect the musculoskeletal system, the network of muscles, bones, ligaments, and tendons.

- Brain cells are damaged and an overabundance of free radicals are released into the body, causing cellular oxidation that is at the core of all deteriorating body tissue and aging. These free radicals cause your cells to mutate into cancer.

In Ayurveda, uncontrolled stress is seen as blocking the flow of prana, or the life-force energy that travels through us and around us. According to Ayurveda, stress negatively affects the central nervous system, blood chemistry, and the cardiovascular, hormonal, respiratory, gastrointestinal, and immune system functions.

So no exaggeration here, my friends: Stress *can and does* kill.

Our creativity, our joie de vivre, and our love for our fellow human beings all suffer when we are in the throes of stress. It can transform us from calm, compassionate, joyful human beings into fiery rage-a-holics, jumpy scaredy-cats, or depressed and moody couch potatoes.

Assess Your Stress

Ask yourself, do you process the stress in your own sphere of influence—whether at home, work, or during your leisure time—well? Do you have great coping skills? Your day may involve a packed-tight schedule, interaction with a wide variety of personality types and energies, and many decisions that require your full brainpower and all of your creativity. You may also be moving your body through a wide range of postures and positions (or, conversely, not moving much at all!)—along with the possibilities of scant or poor nutrition, environmental toxicity, and compromised sleep—which can all have a dramatic impact on your mind-body physiology and energy levels. *If you let it.*

Life holds the potential for layer upon layer of stressors—the dance of relationships; paying bills; running a household; losing loved ones; caring for children or aging parents; illnesses; the news of violence, war, and mayhem; deepening environmental degradation; and most certainly the incredible time crunch to try and fit it all in! Just saying all of this starts my stress hormones flowing! But a few shoulder-releasing yoga asanas, and ten deep diaphragmatic breaths later, I'm cool as a cucumber, I'm one with the universe, *and I've* stopped the damaging flow of stress hormones in their tracks!

Coming into Balance

When we're grounded and coming from a place of balance, our interactions with the whole of life will be from the highest level of consciousness. There is some profound and soulful energy being transmitted during these encounters. In creating these experiences in consciousness, calmness, compassion, enthusiasm, joy, creativity, and intuition are all dramatically enhanced. So, again, it comes back to our attention. Our mindfulness.

Staying "Centered"

Centered (also known as "grounded" or "balanced") in self, you will not founder when life's stressors are brewing around you. By "centering" yourself, you awaken to the truth—to who you really are and why you're here—to the eternal, immortal part of your being. This "I am" consciousness is alive in you, and every one of us has the potential to tap in to it.

We will never be able to eradicate toxic stress from our lives, but we can learn to reduce and manage stressors by changing how we perceive and respond to them. This is where self-knowledge becomes paramount: knowing that we're the choice-makers in our own lives. And to modulate or quell the stress response, we must stay in a place of positivity versus negativity as much as we possibly can. Importantly, however, don't look to escape your shadow. Learn to love yourself there. Let the stress be in you, feel it as much as you can, simply don't fight it. Give it space. Have compassion toward it. Breath through it. Diffuse it. As Zen monk Shunryu Suzuki said, "Keep your front door and your back door open. Allow your thoughts to come and go. Just don't serve them tea."

I know that this is a tall order, but you must *affirm and know that you are in control* of your life. You, and not some external force, are in charge of your destiny. You can get to this place of centeredness, consciously witnessing what you're doing in any given moment, through daily contemplative practices including: prayer, meditation and visualization techniques, positive affirmations, healing breath, and movement. Add optimal nutrition and sensory modulation techniques including massage and aroma, sound, and visual therapies, and you will strengthen your body along with your mind. We will be visiting all of these healing activities in these pages.

Any or all of these practices in combination with each other can dramatically alter consciousness and shift energy to a higher vibrational realm where transformation and great healing can take place.

I'm reminded of a beautiful ancient saying that I return to time and time again: "In a pure mind, there is constant awareness of self. Where there is constant awareness of self, freedom ends bondage, and joy ends sorrow." *When you have the power to control your reaction to potentially stressful situations, you have the power to diffuse stress's debilitating effects on the mind-body physiology.* Being centered in self will give you this power.

Check Your Stress Levels

The following short list can help you to check your stress levels.

Do you:

☐ Feel tired and lacking in energy more often than you'd like?

☐ Find it hard to control your emotions? Easily becoming anxious, agitated, or even angry when faced with minor problems?

☐ Find it hard to fall asleep? Stay asleep?

☐ Rehash what you shoulda, woulda, coulda done or said? Do you have obsessive thoughts and trouble moving on?

☐ Have feelings of dread and doom?

☐ Have trouble sitting still, concentrating or completing tasks?

☐ Have racing heartbeats, shortness of breath, or chest pain?

☐ Have frequent problems with your gastrointestinal system, including heartburn, constipation, or diarrhea?

☐ Feel frequent musculoskeletal pain in your neck, back, and shoulders?

☐ Have frequent headaches?

☐ Experience nervousness and/or sweat a lot?

☐ Drink alcohol excessively?

If you answered yes to even a few of these questions, it is important for you to take steps to reduce your stress levels.

You Deserve a Break Today

If your stress meter is stuck on high, and your circuits are on overload—it's time to pull back and ask yourself how you might unplug, pause, and press the reset button. Something needs to give. Really reflect on this, and hear what your inner sense is telling you. After all, we are talking about healing here. If you don't know whether you're coming or going, it's only a matter of time before an intervention takes place in some form to get you to slow down. It might be a failed relationship, addictions, an accident, or an illness—or one of a number of possible unpleasantries that might befall you. It's essential that we put ourselves back at the top of our to-do list. Give yourself permission to noodle around a bit. Take back your time. Don't give it all away. In giving ourselves extreme self-care—taking time out to be idle, and even to be a bit hedonistic and indulge—we can go a long way toward expelling stress.

Disconnect from the machines, and spend the day doing nothing. See the glorious wistfulness in your soul. Spend the day dancing to your own internal melody, spinning your radio dial, watching the clouds. Have a pajama day! Go for a long meandering walk with no destination in mind. Lay in the hammock out back and stare at the stars. Watch Swedish adult cinema, or Clint Eastwood's spaghetti Westerns, one after another—whatever floats your boat. Other ideas: schedule "me" time in your calendar, have that afternoon yoga break—a few delicious postures with deep breathing, signaling you to slow down. Call in sick, take a proper tea break—heck, go to a high tea. Sleep, nap, daydream, take a hot bath, take long lunches with friends, have a jog, have sex. Get small tasks done in the week and take the weekend off, just for you, if possible. Make a space for your spirit to be free. I realize we're talking about doing nothing here, but your spontaneous, liberated self is getting rid of the programmed schedule for this little bit of time—and that constitutes doing nothing. Avoid schedules and calendar alerts. Just leave your time open to let whatever happens happen. Let time fall away.

And please keep a positive attitude when you're doing nothing. When you're relaxed, your body is at rest and your mind is open to positive suggestions. If you're obsessing on negative thoughts (especially those that make you feel guilty for being idle), ask yourself if those thoughts are productive. If the answer is no, tell yourself, "Stop! This is not constructive," and refocus your thinking on a positive affirmation. Or, you can visualize. Imagine loading your negative thoughts into a small boat. Watch the boat drift out to sea and sink. Just remember, doing nothing—if you do it with a positive focus and do it regularly—reduces stress, improves functioning and coping skills, boosts self-confidence and worth, and just plain feels good. In fact, it's essential to health and well-being. You will experience tremendous equilibrium—and the most fantastic physical, emotional, and spiritual rejuvenation.

And, lastly, consider reciting the following to yourself each and every morning, and you will go a long way toward deflecting emotional stressors. This is a lovely amalgamation from the works of Dale Carnegie and Deepak Chopra, and *A Course in Miracles*.

Today I make the following commitments:

- I will not criticize, condemn, complain, or judge.

- Every decision I make today will be a choice between a grievance and a miracle.

- I will accept responsibility for what I see, what I choose, and the feelings I experience. I will set goals that I will achieve, and everything that seems to be happening to me I ask for and receive, just as I asked.

Journaling: Let Your Soul Write

A journal is a personal record of the innermost you. This is what you think, feel, and do without the judgment and pressures of others. This is you with *just you* and there's no reason not to tell the truth. When written with honesty, your journal can bring you face-to-face with the truth of yourself. It is simply one of the best self-awareness tools—and is one of my favorite consciousness-raising experiences. It helps you to see where patterns of dissonance or chaos are happening in your life, and perhaps you can adapt to avoid them. That's how we acquire wisdom and grow. Also use your journal to reflect on and have gratitude for the joys that life brings. Make lists of the good things that happened to you that day. Acknowledge all the good in your life as well as the difficult. Revisit the good as often as you can. Life is sweeter when we keep a sense of its wonders close to our heart, all day long.

continues on page 68

Diffusing Stress

This book in its entirety shares practices for managing the stressors in your life. But here is a stream of consciousness list of miscellaneous things that can diffuse stress, create stability, and add greater mindfulness in your life. *And* they'll make you happy! Please do consider making your own stream of consciousness list!

* Practice diaphragmatic or belly breathing to calm and energize simultaneously. It will shift you out of stress mode into relaxation mode within a minute. (See Chapter 8 on breathing.)

* Meditate regularly to open your heart and connect with your source, essence, spirit, core of your being.

* Journal your innermost thoughts to clear/ease the overactive mind.

* Get lots of "playtime" or physical activity—every day—including cardio, strengthening, and flexibility activities.

* Hug, hug, kiss, kiss—get that feel-good love hormone, oxytocin, flowing.

* Laugh loud and often.

* Prepare and eat simple, pure, whole organic foods with a joyous and loving spirit. Stay hydrated.

* Make restful sleep a number one priority—go to bed early and rise early.

* Minimize disturbing influences.

* Enjoy massage/bodywork therapies as often as possible.

* Seek out calming aromas and music.

* Go out into prana-rich nature every day. Breathe in the aromas of growing plants. Hug the trees. Lie in the grass. If you can't go there physically, capture beauty through visualization.

* Don't stress about or base your happiness on things you can't control, like weather, traffic, or other people's behavior.

* Learn, as they say in Taoism, to "go with the flow." Be fluid, soft, gentle, and changeable like flowing water.

* Try to look at all change as a lesson and a positive, expansive experience.

* Enhance relationships through conscious, compassionate communication. Be a deep listener.

* Ask for help from friends, family, or professionals when necessary.*

* Prioritize activities, and so better manage time.

* Take a high-quality multivitamin with antioxidants.

* Consider omega-3 essential fatty acids for brain, heart, and hormonal health.

Slow down and enjoy as many of these stress-reducing and blissful practices as you can.

Please read on, my friends, for more powerful practices and coping strategies for managing stress, healing, and deeply caring for your beautiful, loving self!

*Some of us just don't know what it feels like to relax, or we find we can't commit to popular stress-management practices like meditation, yoga, pranayama, exercise, and the like. If this sounds like you, biofeedback or hypnotherapy may provide the skills to tame the "stress monster" for good—with many top integrative physicians touting the benefits, including Andrew Weil, Dr. Oz, Deepak Chopra, and others. These techniques are very empowering and show us that we have the ability to gain control over our mind-body physiology, such as life challenges in the here and now, as well as buried emotional trauma.

It helps you to identify the why, who, when, and where of your experiences, along with the accompanying emotions, to bring circumstances into clear focus—those you're thankful for, or perhaps your fears, or areas where you lack self-confidence or fortitude to follow through. To help you do this, keep a journal every day. Write down whatever is on your mind—from the most mundane to the most bizarre thoughts and everything in between. This will prove tremendously cathartic for your soul, as it allows you to clear out the gunk, vent your feelings, and, along the way, make some important self-discoveries. For instance, you will probably spot the repetition of thoughts. These are areas in your life that may need extra attention. Try to write a few passages every day.

If struggling with a particular issue, it's especially good to have your journal handy. Write a few words about what's going on. Note your feelings and the sensations that these feelings create in your body and mind. If you're in the midst of a difficult experience, talk it through—just you and your journal. And certainly if you experience any form of fulfillment, exhilaration, love, and gratitude, note this, as well. Acknowledging good feelings allows you to more readily see and feel the love and grace around you and thus become an expression of this love and grace. You're writing the story of your life in your journal's pages, and the process of writing brings your experiences fully into your consciousness, all a part of reaching your full human potential.

Progressive Relaxation:
A Classic Practice to Relieve Tension in the Mind-Body Physiology

It's been estimated that we have 60,000 thoughts a day, 59,000 of them reruns from the day before. That's a lot of goop clogging up the system, wouldn't you say? In Eastern philosophy, they call this *monkey mind*. The following is a classic yet simple practice for bringing you back into your body and out of your monkey mind, quicker than you can say, "relaxation response." And indeed that's what this is widely used for: to elicit the relaxation response. We have become such conditioned bundles of reflexes in the mind-body physiology. Hear a beep, react. An essential part of learning how to relax involves learning to pay close attention to the feelings of both tension and relaxation in our bodies.

This technique teaches us to become aware of tension in the body and how to release it.

1. Sit or lie in a comfortable position. Close your eyes, and breathe rhythmically in and out.

2. Begin at the crown of your head. Focus on this area for several seconds. Notice the tension through the scalp, and give yourself permission to let it go. Just let it go. Breathe several breaths, noticing the feeling of body tissues relaxing. Move onward to the forehead and face, doing the same. Let your shoulders melt down away from the ears; release your jaw. Also, remember to soften the inner body.

3. Progressively move your attention from the top of your head to the tips of your toes, checking in on your body, tightening body tissues and then releasing any tension. Remember to breathe! Move through the neck; shoulders; the front torso; the arms, hands, fingers; the spinal column; the upper, middle, lower back; the buttocks; the pelvic area; the thighs; the hamstrings; the calves and the legs, feet, toes—tightening and then releasing tension in each area of the body. As you direct your mind to releasing tension in the body, the idea is that the mind will release tension as well.

4. Having moved along the entire body in this way, pay close attention. Is there any place that needs additional work? Return there, and consciously breathe into this area, releasing tension on the exhale. When you feel completely at ease, slowly bring your THOUGHTS back to the present.

You may use this practice anytime, anywhere. Serenity now!

....

embracing mindfulness

*Ten times a day something happens to me like this—some strengthening
throb of amazement—some good sweet empathic ping and swell.
This is the first, the wildest and the wisest thing I know: that the soul exists
and is built entirely out of attentiveness.*

—POET MARY OLIVER

Are you mind-full or mindful? There's a tremendous difference.
In a mind-full state, we dwell on past thoughts and "chatter," fail-
ing to live in the moment (this is often called *monkey mind*, as we
discussed in the last chapter). Mindfulness, on the other hand, is
a way of being that we methodically develop through contemplative
practices like meditation and yoga. Mindfulness is the nonjudgmental awareness, or "witnessing," of the moment and our place
in it, also referred to as "paying attention on purpose." Training
ourselves to be present to and aware of what's going on inside us
and around us through a regular mindfulness practice leads to
wide-ranging benefits that far exceed the practices themselves. As
we become more present to the consciousness-based layer of our
being, we make more life-affirming choices.

In my work, I regularly teach meditation. I also teach mindfulness practice. People often confuse the two. What's the difference? Meditation is a dedicated practice that will in part hone our concentration skills, as well as develop our ability to observe our compulsive mind and mental chatter without getting caught up in it. (See Chapter 7 for more information about meditation.)

Mindfulness, the accepting awareness of whatever arises in the senses and in the present moment, is when we use the skill we develop while meditating during our "non-meditating" time.

With mindfulness, it's not a matter of what's happening, but how we relate to what's happening. We're mindful of everything that arises in the senses—joy and sorrow, pleasure and pain, beauty and ugliness, peace and chaos. Mindfulness helps us to break out of our well-worn habitual reactions so we can see everything anew. The experience of mindfulness is vibrant, electrifying, enlivening. Any stale perceptions or limiting reactions have no place in one's mindfulness practice. "Beginner's mind" is an elemental part of this (see Chapter 5).

Many of us strive to be mindful in all our activities, but it can be quite the challenge. Most of the day, we're following our minds wherever they lead us—juggling a wide variety of stimuli, multitasking, dwelling on the past, stressing about the future, telling ourselves stories that aren't true, and so on. Our dedicated practice of meditation hones our skill and adeptness at being more present, more mindful. We practice to thrive or excel in so many facets of our lives—be it relationships, work, school, sports. Meditation is *the* practice for becoming more mindful, whatever our endeavors. When you are fully and nonjudgmentally engaged with the present moment instead of following the mind's distracting thoughts, it increases your appreciation and gratitude for everything you do.

Meditation is by far the most important practice for preventing the mind from controlling us. It empowers us to maintain responsibility for our peace and personal happiness. The more practiced you become through your meditation practice to mindfully live in the moment, the closer you come to living it as a new way of being. And, yes, eventually you'll be able to live it twenty-four seven and 365 days a year.

Diving into Our Depths: Mindfulness vs. Mindlessness

As Leonard Cohen said, "If you don't become the ocean, you'll be seasick every day."

When we live on the surface of life, we allow our inner state to depend on outer circumstances, however erratic they may be. Navigating life in this way can be exhausting and even sicken us. Know that storms will continue to roll in throughout life, creating instability. When we consciously live our lives from our depths—the layer of our being that is pure consciousness—we flow through life with the understanding that the present moment is all we have and things are happening just as they should, right here and right now. So how do we do it? We use every experience we encounter to build more mindfulness into our lives, which ultimately grounds us in our true nature, our true essence of heart-centered love and connectedness to the whole of creation. We will only find this in the present moment, the only moment that is guaranteed to us. There is a wonderful saying about this from A. A. Milne, author of *Winnie the Pooh*, who writes, "Yesterday is history, tomorrow is a mystery, but today is a gift. That's why we call it the present."

As we grow our presence and ability to live from the calm, centered layer of our souls, we will still have to navigate the circumstances and people around us. That will never change. But as we show up and get better at being in the moment, the opportunities to practice allow us to become master navigators throughout our lives, managing stress, maintaining our sense of equanimity and resilience and our passion for life and naturally creating wholeness in mind, body, and soul. The philosopher Pascal said, "There is pleasure in being in a ship beaten about by a storm, when we are sure that it will not founder." Exquisitely present and grounded in spirit, we become a vessel that will not founder as it carries us through life.

Becoming the Witness

When Buddha was asked, "What do you and your followers practice?" he answered, "We sit, we walk, we eat."

Perplexed, the questioner asked "Doesn't everyone sit, walk, and eat?"

"Yes," replied Buddha, "but when we sit, we know we're sitting. When we walk, we know we're walking. When we eat, we know we're eating."

This parable is the heart of mindfulness in our lives: the "witnessing" of the present moment and our place in it, often referred to as "paying attention on purpose." We accept this moment as it is without judgment. When we learn to focus on the here and now and move through it without getting caught up in circular thinking, future worries and past regrets.

Heaven is here where we are and we devote our souls to the minutiae of our daily lives. Whether you're eating a meal, washing dishes, brushing your teeth, making love, sitting in a traffic jam, working hard at the office, navigating a difficult relationship, or caring for an ailing loved one, be aware of the all elements of the experience. What are the facts? How did you feel? How did you react? All parts of the experience and your perception of it can impact your mind-body health in profound ways.

Yes, mindfulness enhances your appreciation of the simplest as well as the most profound of everyday experiences. Each moment becomes sacred. Each moment becomes an opportunity to focus attention on healing, life-affirming choices.

When mindful, we stop resisting life and let moments arise as they are, without labeling them. When we're not mindful, life becomes less satisfying; you're usually somewhere else, wondering what's missing, but in fact, *you're* what's missing. As modern wise men say, "Life is what happens to you while you're busy making other plans." Imagine being with a group of friends as a beautiful sunset unfolds. Everyone except you feels the glorious view. You're busy with your thoughts from the day, plans for tomorrow, your phone, and so on. Rather than observing the sunset, you've let the moment's richness pass you by.

In a balanced life, mindfulness prevents the fabric of our lives—a series of moments—from rushing past in a blur. Rather, we learn to savor each moment, much as we did as children, when the days *and moments* seemed deliciously long. Remember those? As adults, we're in our heads making store and to-do lists, while children are ever present to what's happening right here and right now. For example: We might go into the yard and think, "That grass really needs cutting." Or, "We need rain." Or, "I need to wash the windows." A young child will excitedly point to the sky and say, "Hey, look at that cloud. It looks like a dog," or, "Come over here and look at this ant— he's carrying a piece of dirt that looks like a boulder!" Or, while washing dishes, your mind is everywhere but on the experience at hand, whereas a child might say, "Look at those bubbles, watch them sparkle! They're fun!" You get the idea. Mindfulness encourages us to connect with our inner child. Mindfulness will allow you to explore how the bubbles feel, how they pop when hit with water, the way they shine in the kitchen light. We can then experience our lives with exuberance and joy . . . this is the epitome of mindful curiosity.

Our pet companions are also excellent teachers. It never fails to amaze me how present our dogs are on our walks, for example. They may smell a blade of grass for a minute, running their nose up and down all sides while sniffing. There is a universe in that blade of grass, and by golly they're experiencing it! Or they'll gaze at the hawk soaring overhead on the tailwinds until it's no longer in view. I in turn stop and gaze with them, reminding myself to "be here now." Again, they are excellent teachers. There's no agenda there other than pure attention and enjoyment in the moment.

And, by the way, this would also very much be our modus operandi in less inspired moments—difficult, painful, dissonant, chaotic moments—to make them lessons or *blessons* (the realization that our suffering, pain, and challenges are both lessons and blessings) that we may learn from. When we are mindful, we don't try to push these feelings away, but rather sit with and experience them, before intending to release them. We don't judge, label, or identify with them—we just watch these fleeting thoughts come and go. And through it all, unconditionally love yourself—wounds, scars, warts, and all. Each time we unabashedly show up to our essence in this way, we're living, breathing, and expanding into higher vibratory realms of existence where our light becomes stronger and undeniable. Our wounds and scars can always function as openings to spirit if we allow this to happen. Truly, as one of my favorite poets Rumi said, "The wound is the place where the Light enters you." Mindfulness allows for this sacred experience to unfold.

If you're fully present as each moment unfolds, your life changes dramatically, with the potential to become vibrant and electrifying beyond compare. You see the fullness of what is, rather than what's lacking—engendering a profound sense of gratitude.

Being fully present also brings with it the knowledge required to make good choices during stressful situations. Yes, mindfulness encourages you to consciously work with your own stress, pain, illness, and everyday challenges instead of simply "stuffing" them into your subconscious. With mindfulness, even the most disturbing thoughts, feelings, and experiences can be viewed from a wider perspective as passing events in the mind, rather than as "us," or as necessarily being true. As we become skilled at observing our thoughts, breathing with them, allowing them to happen without judging, believing, arguing, or interacting with them, we become more accepting of them. This results in less distressing feelings, and increases our ability to enjoy our lives.

Trying to control our thoughts is such a poor use of our energy and time. Rather, let's intend that our thoughts not control us. Practice cultivating awareness of your thoughts, skillfully observing them without getting caught up in their details. As you do this, you learn to interrupt conditioned behavior—the habitual reactivity to our thoughts. Without awareness, the compulsive nonstop dialogue going on in our heads leads to so much emotional reactivity. Observing our thoughts allows us to interrupt this process, to learn not to attach to them or get swept away by them. We learn to see our thoughts for what they are: temporary fluctuations of energy and information. They come and go like clouds floating by through the sky. The same holds true for our emotions. When we dwell or wallow in them, our reactive, conditioned response will inevitably kick in. Mindfulness can short-circuit these conditioned responses.

So many mindlessly go through their days on autopilot, with the mind's incessant chatter and control dramas creating the perfect breeding ground for stress, anxiety, worry, fear, depression, and self-doubt. Regular mindfulness practice helps us to see our thoughts and emotions for what they are—the constantly changing landscape of our mind. The more you practice, the better you'll get at carrying this mindfulness into every facet of your life. And with this, your overall sense of well-being and life satisfaction dramatically improve.

We may often be distracted by the persistent needs of the ego: the need for power, control, approval—the need to judge. Spirit doesn't have any of those needs. Spirit just is, right now, in this moment. Meditation—and by extension mindfulness—connects you to spirit, and when it does, you make the most life-affirming choices for yourself rather than those from learned habits, physical needs, or addictions. For example, consider how you wake up. Do you bolt out of bed and stumble to the shower, barely aware of the time, date, or century? To witness your own morning and nurture your life-force energy, wake up slowly. Make awakening a delightful ritual. Do a bit of yoga (even in bed!), enjoy a moment of meditation, practice self-massage, step in the shower and become one with the water. As you move through your day, greet people in a nonjudgmental and compassionate way. Mindfulness will transform your every moment of every day!

Mindfulness Cues Can Help

Mindfulness is you paying attention and being present and at peace. Our ability to stay with and in the moment is essential to seeing, hearing, learning, and realizing a deeper acceptance of all things.

Each day, countless events pull us off our intention to be in the moment, causing our minds to wander. When you notice your mind wandering, chose a word or phrase to bring you back to the now. That awareness of the moment, whether you are turning on a shower or pulling out your cell phone, takes on a meditative quality in real time. That feeling brings peace. Every time you undertake a small action, take a deep breath. Oxygen fills the body, relaxing the muscles and clearing unnecessary thoughts from your mind.

Transitions in your day are the perfect time to reset mindfulness. Say you have to make an important telephone call. Sit down, roll your shoulders, and take a few deep breaths. Think about your intentions for the exchange. Smile. Dial. You'll be amazed at the difference in outcomes than had you rushed the conversation to get on to the next task. By slowing down, you become more available for the exchange. You have given yourself time to process and think—and you have given the other person that same courtesy, increasing the potential for success!

Throughout this process, pay attention to your beating heart. That rhythm is your rhythm. If your mind races up the path before your heart, everything is out of rhythm. Your brain is moving too fast and you'll miss something! Get back in sync when this happens. Listen to your heartbeat while taking deep, energizing breaths. Focus your attention on that heartbeat and pairing it with oxygen flow.

Just as you may zone out during a telephone call, you also tend to zone out during the daily tasks we all do day in and day out: showering, driving, eating, sleeping. Every day may feel repetitive. Trust me, it's not. Each day is different by a countless number or variables, even if it is not apparent to the human psyche. Transform the experience by simply being present.

Say you are having your morning shower. Focus on the water, how it feels as it hits and flows down the body. Feel the temperature and how it makes your body feel. How does the soap smell on your skin? Does your scalp tingle as you work the shampoo into your scalp? Is it relaxing? By simply registering the sensations of each shower, it becomes a new—and wonderful—experience.

 ## Mindfulness Practice

Though mindfulness takes practice, as with forming any new habit it can become second nature. Some common wisdom says it takes twenty days to form a new habit, and mindfulness is no exception! Just take that time to witness your thoughts from when you get up in the morning until you go to bed at night. Narrate your day to yourself: "Good morning, self," and so on; do so with great interest and enthusiasm.

Cultivate and practice noticing what gets your attention and what you usually ignore. To paraphrase Jesus, where your attention is, there will your heart be also. If you think about what you paid attention to throughout your day, what did you learn about yourself? What place did love and soulful connection with others have in your day? Would you like to change where you put your attention, time, and concern? These are all important questions for the soul that wants awareness.

A more formal approach to mindfulness is through meditation with a particular focus on breathing. Sit in a chair with shoulders relaxed, or lie on your back. Keep your spine straight. Focus on every aspect of your breathing, the gentle in and out of air. "Be with"—follow it with body and mind as it travels up and down the body—each in-breath and out-breath for its full duration, as if you're riding the waves of your own breathing. You may feel the coolness of the breath as you inhale through your nostrils. Fill your lungs as widely and deeply as is comfortable for you on the in-take. You'll feel your belly gently rise and expand. The belly then falls or lowers on the exhale. Make certain you fully exhale before taking in the next breath. A slight pause after the inhale and after the exhale allows you to feel the entire fullness and lightness of each in-and-out. Feel the warmth of the air through your nostrils as you fully exhale. Feel it all and take note.

Every time you notice that your mind has wandered away from watching your breath, notice what took you away, and then gently bring your attention back to your breathing. It's okay and natural for thoughts to arise and distractions carry your attention away to follow them. Simply accept them without judging, labeling, or interacting with them. Just let them come and go like cars on the street or sunlight patterns on the floor. Now bring your attention back to the breath. Send yourself healing, loving energy through this process. Breathe it all in, love it all out!

If your mind wanders away from the breath a hundred times, then your job is simply to bring it back to the breath every time, no matter what it becomes preoccupied with. Continue this way for several minutes, ultimately working up to fifteen minutes per day. Over time, you will become grateful for your mindfulness meditation time. You'll look forward to it.

Jon Kabat-Zinn, a mentor of mine in the mindfulness practice space, is the creator/founder of the Mindfulness-Based Stress Reduction (MBSR) program, which helps people cope with stress, PTSD, anxiety, pain, and illness. This esteemed program is offered at medical centers, hospitals, and health maintenance organizations worldwide.

As Kabat-Zinn is fond of saying, "You can't stop the waves, but you can learn to surf." He often uses the example of waves to explain mindfulness.

"Think of your mind as the surface of a lake or ocean. There are always waves on the water, sometimes big, sometimes small, sometimes almost imperceptible. The water's waves are churned up by the winds, which come and go and vary in direction and intensity, just as do the winds of stress and change in our lives, which stir up waves in our mind. It's possible to find shelter from much of the wind that agitates the mind. Whatever we might do to prevent them, the winds of life and of the mind will blow." *

....

*Portions of this section were first published in *Organic Spa Magazine*, "Embracing Mindfulness," July 1, 2014.

5

new beginnings with "beginner's mind"

In the beginner's mind there are many possibilities, in the expert's mind there are few.
—SHUNRYU SUZUKI

Writer R. J. Rim said, "I found a way to see in the dark. Close your eyes." This expresses the Zen practice of beginner's mind beautifully—an excellent addition to your mindfulness practice. Turn off the "lights," open your mind, drop into your heart, and see with new eyes. Whatever you're striving toward—turning a new leaf, starting a new chapter, heightened well-being, enhanced relationships, dropping prejudices or old beliefs—beginner's mind may just be the answer.

Human nature can be so fickle. We know what's good for us— we're inundated with stress management guidance at every turn— yet we let our resolutions to be better and do better fall by the wayside. Why? Is it boredom? Is it self-improvement fatigue? A lack of patience? Maybe the timing isn't right. Or we simply don't want to do anything too daunting. But life-altering change takes effort. Enter beginner's mind, an attitude that anyone can culti-vate with practice. This mind-set allows us to revisit, comprehend, or appreciate any and all information with new eyes. It refers to having an attitude of openness and eagerness, along with a lack of preconceptions about intentions, working toward new goals, learning new terrain (and revisiting the old).

Here's the Secret Sauce

Beginner's mind is in essence playful curiosity. Mindfulness and curiosity make for a lovely partnership. While mindfulness is pay-ing attention to the moment with compassion and no judgment, curiosity is stoked to dive in deeper and unearth new discoveries about what's being noticed. So a cool part of this is that as we're developing greater awareness of our self and our world, we're also learning. What a way to stay engaged with our miraculous life here on this earthly plane!

Lifelong learning is one of the most effective ways to deal with change, and change is ever constant—change in our personal and professional lives, change in our communities, and change in our world. In fact, the only thing that doesn't change is change! Expect it! Change is a constant in all life. Well-educated indi-viduals make for a better society for all of us. Lifelong learners are happier, healthier, and live longer. Peter Drucker, one of the most influential management educators and authors, said, "We now accept the fact that learning is a lifelong process of keeping abreast of change. And the most pressing task is to teach people how to learn." Practicing a beginner's mind-set definitely gives you an advantage in the learning arena. A commitment to lifelong learning leads to expanded levels of consciousness about our true nature, about others, and about our world. Science has proven this wisdom correct with a new field of study called "neuroplasticity." If you learn new information, better methods, or experience a change in your perception, your brain circuits (or hardware, for lack of a better word) form new neuron pathways. You rewire and change as you go. When we're interested, our relationships, our life, our world, and by extension our sweet loving selves become oh-so-interesting. And this never stops, even into old age. You have the tools to keep your brain healthy by just using it. Such a beautiful feedback loop!

Stepping into the Unknown: The Field of Infinite Possibilities

"Being at ease with not knowing is crucial for answers to come to you."
—Eckhart Tolle

"I am the wisest man alive, for I know one thing, and that is that I know nothing."
—Socrates

Beginner's mind consciously sets aside a know-it-all mind-set that diminishes enthusiasm and undervalues the tried and true. A beginner's mind is fond of saying, "There might just be more here than meets the eye. There might be something here that I've missed. Let's have another look." There is an almost childlike innocence and wonderment to it—an openness to possibility. It encourages us to take everything we know including our opinions, preconceived notions, and, yes, even our cherished beliefs and put them away for just a bit. I teach Deepak Chopra's Seven Spiritual Laws of Success (see appendix), of which the Law of Detachment is integral to our achieving true freedom. It states, "In detachment lies the wisdom of uncertainty . . . in the wisdom of uncertainty lies the freedom from our past, from the known, which is the prison of past conditioning. And in our willingness to step into the unknown, the field of all possibilities, we surrender ourselves to the creative mind that orchestrates the dance of the universe."

Beginner's mind encourages us to step into the unknown—to say, "I don't know," even if you think you know. "I know" prevents us from understanding the present moment's mysteries, and keeps us living in the past. With this, we can easily become cynical, jaded, complacent, or unmotivated. We close ourselves off to the spontaneous, to the unexpected—to the discoveries and surprises that give life such zest! So just throw up your hands and say, "I don't know!" Not knowing is a wonderful state to be in, so innocent and liberating. Beginner's mind knows that even in the most familiar circumstances, there are riches to be unearthed. This is exploration of the deepest and most powerful kind. This is an odyssey into the terrain of self, really—and by extension, one's universe. You think you know your significant other? How about your children? How about your mom? How about your boss? How about your community? Your world? How about *yourself*? I promise you that there's so much more there to discover. You can glance along the surface or really delve in deep, where infinite possibilities reside.

Lao Tzu said: "Not-knowing is true knowledge. Presuming to know is a disease. First realize that you are sick; then you can move toward health. The Master is her own physician. She has healed herself of all knowing. Thus she is truly whole."

An important life lesson is that people who think they already know, know nothing. We often think we know so much. (Especially in this era of "alternative facts"!) How often have you found yourself saying, "I know, I know." I have. Of course, none of us really knows it all. We presume to know. Consequently, we miss out on a whole lot that life could teach us, if only we were willing to learn. Become your own physician. Heal yourself of any presumption. Realize, as I did, that you know far less than you ever could imagine. I still have so much to unlearn. I unlearn every day by practicing saying, "I don't know." The more I unlearn and the more I realize I don't know, the more I learn and the more I know. But I am always on my guard, because if there is one thing I have learned, it is that presuming to know keeps me from learning more. I am on the path to wholeness and I still know nothing—God, I love this beginner's mind!

Spiritualize Your Relationships

In forming lasting relationships, mindfulness coupled with beginner's mind leads to a heightened awareness of our attitudes and behaviors toward those we perceive as different from us, whom we may hold any prejudice toward. It encourages us to explore beyond any differences, find common ground, and bond through our found and shared similarities. And for those with whom we're already simpatico, it encourages us to go ever deeper, to find our unique and fascinating differences to learn about and feast on together. This can form some of the most deeply bonded friendships. Ever. Ultimately we become more aware of all those we are in relationship with and, while we're at it, reach a deeper understanding of ourselves.

Beginner's mind allows you to see your world anew every day so that, in every moment, old information can reach you in new ways, bringing fresh insights. Naturally, as you nurture or embody beginner's mind in the midst of relationships, conscious communication is an integral part of this. And it includes deep, active listening of the highest order. In relation to self and others, our belief system often wants to stand its ground. This is the puffed-up ego in charge, with the need for control, the need for approval, the need for power, the need to judge. I encourage you to be present. Surrender. Let it go. Repeat after me: "I don't know." And then listen.

 Let's Practice

Living mindfully along with the regular practice of meditation, intention, visualization, and positive affirmations will all be beneficial in cultivating your beginner's mind. Open up to your "I don't know" mind and release any predisposition toward judging. Release the common sense, the rational mind, the "I should" mind. Instead, engage in the expansive spirit of inquiry, of questioning rather than looking for answers.

Poet Rainer Maria Rilke said, "Be patient toward all that is unsolved in your heart and try to love the questions themselves, like locked rooms and like books that are now written in a very foreign tongue. Do not now seek the answers, which cannot be given you because you would not be able to live them. And the point is, to live everything. Live the questions now. Perhaps you will then gradually, without noticing it, live along some distant day into the answer."

Be gentle, go slowly, and take one day and, yes, even one moment at a time in developing your own beginner's mind. This takes practice and nurturing. Carefully watch when the inner know-it-all rears its ugly head and bring your attention to that part of your being where infinite possibilities reside, to spirit.

Meditation is integral in fostering a beginner's mind; it newly inspires us, gets our creative juices flowing, and jump-starts positive change. It helps to de-emphasize the old programming that replays over and over again in our minds, driving our unconscious behavior—while emphasizing positive thoughts and emotions. And on that note, use positive self-talk often. When you get up in the morning, look in the mirror and say to yourself, "Every day in every way, I'm getting better and better." Or, "Today's a new day, and I can walk a different path." Ultimately, no matter what you're striving for, no matter what the situation or experience, intend on receiving value from it. Just remember that energy follows intention.

If being more present and curious about self, others, places, experiences, or things helps us to develop greater fondness, tenderness, caring, and, in essence, humanity, then what are we waiting for? By adding beginner's mind to our mindfulness practice we ensure our continued development as kind, compassionate, generous, and happy individuals who are engaged in our world with wonderment and love.

....

6

the power of intention

Our intention creates our reality.

—WAYNE DYER

Intentionality is married to mindfulness. If you want to change some aspect of your life, direct your mind toward a goal, or manifest your dreams, start by setting an intention—making the deliberate decision to create something or intend that something will happen. Intentions aren't fleeting thoughts or wishes, but, rather, they're like divine jet fuel—turning your good but half-baked ideas into glorious, wholly formed bullet points. They allow you to visualize and clarify what matters most to you. Intentions help you to "jack up" your commitment level, whatever the undertaking—be it meditating daily; being kind; spending more quality time with loved ones or alone; getting healthy and physically fit; working toward a new career you're passionate about; working less and playing more; learning something new—you get the idea. An intention can recast a budding thought into a driving desire. It will laser your focus to act with fierce clarity, to psyche yourself up for a major campaign to cut the noise, the nonsense—so that your radiant essence can shine.

Intention is one of the most profound practices to inspire, enthuse, experience joy—to stay the course. You can set an intention anytime, anywhere. It's powerful to focus your awareness on an intention before any form of contemplative practice. Then you'll be operating from a place of fluidity and calm assurance where intuition, intelligence, and sensory perception are heightened.

No doubt, intentions can assist you in taking greater control over your life. Many people get up in the morning and move through their day with no inkling as to what they want to accomplish or what they want their day to hold. I call this "flying by the seat of your pants!" Conversely, many of us just stumble along after our "habit mind," mechanically and mindlessly following the exact same path and programming day after day. With intent, you verbalize to yourself what you want to create for yourself or how you want to feel, and by so doing, you program your subconscious to achieve your dreams and transform your being—mind, body, and soul—in wondrous ways.

Setting an intention can be as simple as saying, "I feel grounded," or, "I am joyous," or, "I am courageous." Or, it can be as detailed as that of sweet Bessie—who set an intention at seventy years old to become a world-renowned photographer. Although many thought her too old, she didn't. She vividly kept her intent and burning desire alive in her mind's eye. She entered a national photo contest where she won the first prize of $10,000. Her prize-winning photo toured the world with a Kodak exhibit. As Bessie said, "We're never too old to make our dreams come true." We're never *too anything* to make our dreams come true!

Intention can also help in creating a powerful energetic shift away from feeling trapped or victimized. No matter how challenging a situation may be, there is always a way to move forward. When you can visualize and verbalize a positive outcome, you cannot help but move toward it.

Tony Robbins says, "Where focus goes, energy flows." Exactly! Or my version, "Energy follows intention." The key in all of this is to follow your intention with an action that supports the intention. All this dynamic energy is then flowing in the same direction. If you consistently do this, you will experience quick results and feel good and harmonious in the process. And naturally, if you set an intention, but the energy surrounding your action is flowing in a different direction, then an undesirable outcome is more likely to result along with the inherent stress, and emotions such as anxiety, sadness, or anger. Let's look at an example: If your intention is to improve your relationship with your significant other and your action is to start a productive conversation, check in with a phone call or email during the day, or give a shoulder rub, then improving your relationship is highly probable. However, if the energy of your actions is in opposition to your intent—coming home late without a phone call or explanation, verbal abuse, ignoring them—then the opposing energies will cause friction and stress. So we're thriving to set an intention, then direct our energy toward that desired outcome through our actions. Harmony, balance, and manifestation of our desires will result.

Take the mantra "energy follows intention" and make it yours. Apply it to things you want to change. Meditate on these intentions, write each down, and consider how you might adjust certain attitudes and behaviors that influence outcomes. Do you feel your energy focused on what you hope to achieve? So many people want to change—and have excellent intentions—but fail to get the outcome they seek. It takes mindfulness, awareness of what you want, and then a direction of your energies to make that change happen. Lip service to a list of unrealized New Year's Resolutions won't work. (I call this endless resetting of intention "self-improvement fatigue" or "boredom.") This approach breeds frustration because actions do not meet intentions. What you intend does not match what you actually do, creating friction. Know your intention and match your actions to it. It's that simple: Intention plus focused energy = change.

The key in aligning your worldly actions with your inner values lies in your intent—and specifically with your intention statement. (Remember, your "intention statement" is your point of focus, the shape you put on the change you would like to experience. For example, my intention statement might be "I want to show more kindness to the people in my life." Your path is the loving-kindness meditation with a focus on positive, supportive thoughts, words and deeds.) The words you use to verbalize your intention amplify the power of thought, creating an energetic imprint. Again, this is all about energy. Our nervous system hears and responds to an intention statement clearly focused on the intent. For example: To say, "I intend to do whatever it takes to feel relaxed and happy today," is very clear and focused on how your actions can support your well-being. This is preferable to using the words, "I hope to _____, " where you almost give yourself permission to fall short of your goal, or, "I want to _____," where you're too attached to a method of achieving it. Both are wishy-washy! Play around with these three statements for what you want to create in your life, and you'll experience the difference yourself. A properly constructed intention statement puts your attention on the ever-present now in the constantly changing flow of life. Intentions are your inner pilot light—they help activate your inner power.

Mindfulness when coupled with intention is a powerful practice that allows you to become the creator of your own life—inspiring and opening you to the infinite possibilities here on this earthly plane. Together, these two modalities encourage you to choose your values, dreams, and goals; to "see" and positively feel your sense of purpose in being here; and then to go forward to enact a life of meaning and enjoyment. You're now on your path toward fulfilling your dharma—your reason for being.

Go with the Flow

To help yourself positively intend and affirm beautiful, brilliant abundance for your elf, for others, and for your life, try imagining life as a river of energy and information that is forever changing, growing, and expanding. As the great Greek philosopher Heraclitus said, via a translation by Plato, "Everything changes and nothing remains still . . . and . . . you cannot step twice into the same stream." Remember that "the stream"—you and your life and everything around you—is constantly changing. Connecting with amazing new experiences and discoveries in our lives may mean releasing certain constraints or fears that are holding us back—or concerns that prevent us from seeing or accepting something new.

Most common fears stem from a general fear of change. Fears can be strong, and letting go will probably be a gradual process. At first, you may only be able to peek through your doubt, like dipping one toe into the river. Eventually, though, you can overcome any fear—including fear of failure, commitment, disapproval, or success. One day, you'll wake up with an overwhelming desire to plunge into the river and go with the flow. And as you're flowing down this ever-changing river-of-life, if new channels and tributaries of experience present themselves to you, your intentions may morph and change into something new or different. And that's okay. Your intentions are not ironclad. Nothing is written in stone.

If we connect to our essence, our source, our spirit, we can manifest all we desire and learn to work through change positively—fears be damned. We have the power to become the mystic, the sage, the shaman, playing without fear in this extremely fluid and changeable world.

Why Share an Intent?

We truly believe in the power of intentions. After all, every action starts with an intention. When we share an intention with others, we make ourselves feel more accountable for the mission we want to complete. When you know what your intention is and you can state it to others, then you are more likely to make the initiative to make your aspiration come true.

If you want to change your thinking, heal your heart. That's the best meditation of all.

Please do consider visiting intent.com, where you can join a like-minded "intentional" community where members share their dreams and aspirations and receive support from others. Mallika Chopra, the founder and CEO of Intent.com, says, "My intent is to connect with others by sharing and listening to each other's stories."

Mallika learned about the power of intention at a young age from her father, Deepak Chopra. After family meditations, which she learned when she was nine, her father would guide Mallika and her brother, Gotham, to repeat the following phrase, adapted from *A Course in Miracles*:

I am responsible for what I see.

I choose the feelings I experience

And set the goals I will achieve.

Everything that seems to happen to me

I ask for and receive as I have asked.

He taught them to then ask for love, hope, purpose, passion, inspiration, and so many other positive qualities in their lives every day. Starting every day with an intent proved to be an anchoring device that led to connection, happiness, and personal fulfillment.

I highly recommend visiting Mallika's lovely site. This is your online destination for turning your intention into tangible action, and inspiring others to do the same

7

just say om-ward

The quieter you become, the more you can hear.
—RAM DASS

Let us be silent so that we may hear the whispers of God.
—RALPH WALDO EMERSON

Om-Ward Bound

I've shared several aspects of meditation with you during our self-care journey together. Please permit me to dive in a bit deeper here. As I explained in our exploration of mindfulness, a dedicated meditation practice trains your brain to drop into your heart and become present, to become mindful—to "pay attention on purpose." Many of you may already know the deep power of meditation and its ability to help you perceive the beauty, truth, and goodness in your world and your universe. Regardless of where you're at on the spectrum of meditation experience, plug into your beginner's mind and forward ho!

Why Meditate?

Many healers call meditation the ultimate and most important practice for realizing wholeness in mind, body, and spirit.

Through meditation, you'll experience the source of thought—the thinker. This is the real you, spirit. This is the layer of consciousness we discussed earlier called *Atman Darshan*, where we get "a glimpse of the soul." Show up and meditate consistently, and the transformation will be profound. You'll progress to ever higher levels of consciousness, ultimately reaching *moksha,* or pure bliss, a state in which you understand that the field of consciousness that is within you is also universal consciousness. There is no other practice, remedy, treatment, or therapy that can enable you to awaken to your true self like that born of a regular contemplative practice.

Getting Started

To establish a practice—which can be the greatest challenge—you must *want* to meditate, so let's address this first. My greatest wish for each and every one of you reading this chapter (and this book) is that it will serve as the springboard for you to dive in and do this. To want to do it. To intend to do it. Energy follows intention. *A meditation practice is nonnegotiable, period. You just have to do it.* Perhaps the most persuasive argument for meditation is that every spiritual tradition holds a vision of human transformation at its heart. Since meditative practice is essential to spiritual awakening, our shared history points to the practice and affirms its power to make us whole.

Today, we know that meditation is a technology, not some New Age woo-woo. Although it is practiced in all the world's great wisdom traditions, you don't have to adopt a new philosophy or religion to practice it. As far as the medical community goes, it can be as secular a modality as there is for optimal health and well-being.

The scientific research studies of the benefits of meditation for mind-body health are prolific and vigorous. Not only do I now regularly teach meditation to health care professionals of every ilk, but doctors are sending their patients to meditation classes because of meditation's profound ability to manage stress.

No doubt, meditation is a key element of every mind-body health/stress management seminar that I teach, whether at spas, wellness and fitness centers, medical settings, or higher learning settings (standing room only last semester!). In addition, classes are now being offered regularly in fitness/wellness centers, hospitals, schools, corporate offices, and, yes, even prisons. Meditation rooms are regularly seen in airports between prayer chapels and Internet kiosks. Veterans of war are learning about yoga and meditation's powerful healing benefits. I teach yoga and meditation at yearly "Stand Down" events for vets. I even teach meditation to kids in yoga class. One of the world's greatest practitioners said, "If every eight year old in the world is taught meditation, we will eliminate violence from the world in one generation." Amen. What a wonderful vision for our future generations.

The Ultimate Health Care: Meditation

Even though diverse cultures around the world have practiced meditation for thousands of years (talk about empirical knowledge), modern research studies have quantified and qualified meditation's numerous and awe-inspiring benefits for our health. Meditation creates greater brain wave coherence (balances our brain waves), allowing the brain to communicate better with the rest of the body. Meditation allows the brain and the body to calm down enough to work together.

This synchronicity between brain wave patterns also brings greater clarity of thought, clearer memory recall, and enhanced intuition and creativity. Along with quieting down an overactive mind, it lowers blood pressure, slows the heartbeat, and calms the central nervous system. By doing all this, it provides a powerful boost to the immune system. It is used to treat high cholesterol, high blood pressure, headaches, and other acute and chronic illnesses. Our blood vessels even dilate with meditation, and the blocks in our heart vessels actually get smaller, according to the American Heart Association. A study appearing in *Hypertension*, the journal of the American Heart Association, showed normalization of high blood pressure in people who had practiced meditation for only three months. And scientists have now found that those who meditate have a thicker cerebral cortex than those who don't. You grow your gray matter with regular meditation! More brain matter = higher levels of mental acuity/activity. Have I gotten your attention yet? This is a mind-bending, tension-releasing, heart-and-soul-opening practice! But wait, there's more.

Neuroscientists have studied and documented (through some of the most advanced imaging techniques) meditation's effects on rewiring our brain circuitry, where through a knitting together of dissimilar brain circuits (long term when consistently practiced) we become more stress resilient and significantly shift brain waves toward more compassionate and joyful states (dramatic shifts from right prefrontal cortex to left prefrontal cortex, where positive emotions and optimism reside). We spoke of this earlier. Remember the term "neuroplasticity"? Meditation also regulates hormones and increases levels of serotonin, the brain's feel-good neurotransmitter. (Ninety percent of the cells that manufacture serotonin are in the gastrointestinal tract. Another reason to eat well.) And with this, integrative physicians are recommending it for its mental health benefits as well: relieving anxiety and depression (by lowering levels of cortisol), increasing resistance to influences that disturb a person's emotional equilibrium, and assisting with compulsive behaviors and addictions, along with providing better rest and sleep.

Researchers have proved that when we meditate and give our single-pointed focus to one thing, such as our breath or a mantra, the brain restructures itself to make concentration easier. If we practice peaceful acceptance during meditation, our brains become more adaptable/flexible when stressed. If we practice loving-kindness meditation, our brains develop so that we spontaneously feel a deeper connection to others, changing our thoughts, reactions, and actions.

The research is ongoing. However, it's all good. Actually, it's all great news. What we somehow felt, what we intuited, what we practiced for millennia, science has proved true. Sign me up, I'd say!

Silence Is Golden

In meditation, we experience one of life's great favors: silence. When we regularly dive into that gap between our thoughts—where great healing resides—we become more present in each moment of our lives. When we can carve out bits of time throughout the day to intentionally be in silence, we become more present in the moment as living our life. We begin to mindfully (versus mindlessly) make more life-affirming choices and thus sow the seeds that allow us to live a life that is in balance. We hear what is said and what is not said. We heighten our ability to communicate with others, to express ideas creatively, to become a more compassionate and tolerant human being, to unconditionally love both the self and others, and to strive toward the higher meanings in life. In the hyperstimulating, attention deficit times we live in, meditation is a sacred gift that we give to ourselves. It is indeed unfortunate that many will go a lifetime without experiencing this bliss.

Meditation helps us stay in the moment, reduce stress, find inner peace, and remain optimistic even in the face of tremendous challenges. Its practitioners will attest to the many benefits that meditation offers (with longtime meditators feeling these benefits more intensely): peace of mind, a release of tension in the body, deeper concentration, greater mental clarity, increased energy and vitality, heightened optimism, and the ability to act calmly in all situations. The Tao expression "go with the flow" takes on new meaning. Others will not as readily be able to push our buttons and elicit reactions. You will learn to *respond*, rather than react, from a place of balanced, centered spirit.

A dedicated practice is primary for cultivating awareness and developing the skill of observing your compulsive mind and mental chatter *without* indulging or getting caught up in it.

The Meditation Menu

Meditation comes in a variety of flavors: concentrative, passive, mindfulness, loving-kindness, visualization, and movement (walking, yoga, tai chi), along with eating, to name but a few. Many names are given to the various meditation practices, depending on the tradition from which they came. Heightened consciousness is a constant in all these approaches. I honor all of them, but in the interest of space and clarity, I am simplifying here.

I will share one major practice in this chapter: concentrative meditation.

Meditation is truly the most flexible consciousness-raising practice that you could engage in. In its purest form, meditation refers to time spent in quiet introspection. You may go for long walks, do yoga or tai chi, pray, or perform traditional meditation. As long as an activity takes you to a place of calm, a place of heightened awareness and energy, a place of heightened clarity of mind, you are meditating.

In fact, we humans often meditate without even knowing it. Have you ever been absorbed by a beautiful sunset? Have you ever gotten lost in thought while reading a book, gardening, jogging, or even cooking? These are all passive forms of meditation.

Psychologists say that during those "lost" moments our brain waves are similar to those observed during more traditional meditation. While we're in this state, blood pressure drops, the heart rate goes down, and the immune system receives a powerful boost.

In a time-starved, need-for-speed society in which we tend to ignore internal signals, instead letting external signals rule us, it is essential that we give ourselves time to break free and listen to spirit. Meditation is a practice that can bring us to this place, freeing us from the bondage of our egocentricity and the external influences that prevent us from connecting with that pure consciousness layer of our being where infinite possibilities reside.

The Traditional Approach: Concentrative Meditation

Traditional, or what is also called concentrative, meditation is one of the most profound practices for achieving wholeness in mind, body, and spirit.

In this meditation, you give your single-pointed focus to the object of your attention. Your focus may be the repetition of a mantra (meaning an "instrument of the mind") such as *Om* ("eliciting universal peace") or any chosen word or sound. Your focus could also be the simple observation of the breath. Healing breath is a natural bridge to meditation. Or bathe in the layer of your being that is pure consciousness or spirit: the spaceless, timeless, ageless, limitless, and fearless layer of your being that has always been here and will always be—the real you.

One of the most renowned and longtime researchers into the benefits of meditation, Dr. Herbert Benson of the Harvard Medical School, founder of the Benson-Henry Institute for Mind Body Medicine and the author of the classic *The Relaxation Response*, recommends picking a focus word that resonates with you and is soothing. It can be your child's name or a word such as "one," "peace," "love," "shalom," or "amen." *So-hum* (meaning "I am") is a popular mantra that I teach in my classes. "I am spirit." This becomes your personal mantra when you meditate.

The unique vibrational quality of a mantra allows you to take your awareness into a deep inner silence. When this happens, mental

Using a Mantra

A mantra is an instrument of the mind (*man* means "mind," and *tra* means "instrument). This sound-bite world has almost substituted the word "mantra" for mission statement (think "just do it" and "seize the day"), however trivial ("I must find the bag to go with these shoes"). The Yogic tradition, where the word originated, used a Sanskrit symbol for mantra, which is a word or phrase that, once repeated, creates sonic vibrations within our deepest being that trigger and engage deep spiritual experience.

Choose your mantra or get one assigned, as in Transcendental Meditation and Primordial Sound Meditation instruction. (The Chopra Center for Well-Being uses this approach.) If you choose your own, select a word that has meaning for you. Try your children's names, the words "one," "peace," and "love." If you enjoy saying the word and feel the connection to it's meaning, your mantra is all the more powerful.

Your mantra can be used throughout your day to bring you into a more relaxed and present state. Use it.

activity decreases along with overall biochemical activity. Heart and brain wave coherence increases. This gives the body a rest deeper than sleep.

In addition, we train the mind to become more focused, gaining heightened awareness and mental clarity so that we're able to concentrate better and do *anything* more effectively.

Let's Practice: Concentrative Meditation

Try to give yourself the gift of meditation every single day. Personally, I enjoy meditating for twenty minutes at dawn and dusk, the times when our circadian rhythms are most calm and peaceful.

Having said this, let me add that consistency is more important than duration. Begin with a few minutes and build to longer stretches of time as you experience meditation's tremendous benefits. Pretty soon you'll crave your meditation time! During your day, seek to find those minutes, those pockets of peace, when you can infuse your being with the regenerative benefits of meditation.

Choose a place that is quiet and comfortable. If you create a tranquil atmosphere, the mind will soften and focus more readily. If you're in your own personal setting, make this a special place with comfortable cushions to support your body as needed. Create sacred space for your meditation time. Do anything you like to enhance the atmosphere in the place where you go to connect with spirit (for example, candles, gentle ambient background music, incense, or the altar you made in an earlier chapter). Know that as you become a long-term meditator, you will become quite adept at meditating anytime and anywhere.

To calm and center yourself before beginning meditation, consider doing a few minutes of diaphragmatic breathing, alone or coupled with yoga postures. This begins the process of quieting the overactive mind and calming the nervous system.

- Make yourself feel comfortable, preferably with your spinal column in alignment, whether lying down, seated on the floor, or sitting in a chair.

- Close your eyes. Your brain will be more readily able to stop processing information coming from the senses and concentrate.

- Begin saying your mantra or chosen word to yourself. Depending on the mantra, you may say it to yourself on the out-breath. If it has more than one syllable, such as "So hum," you can say "sos" on the inhalation and "hum" on the exhalation. This rhythm helps you focus. Repeat it again and again and again.

- This is where your concentrative efforts take place. If thoughts come into your mind, gently and without judgment watch them come and go like migrating birds or clouds floating through the sky. Now bring your attention back to the repetition of your mantra. The mind may continue to distract you with thoughts. It's not wrong. It's just the nature of the mind. Just keep coming back to what you're focusing on.

- Do this for as long as your time permits, remembering that even a few moments will give you benefits.

You also may choose to simply become aware of your breath. Breathe deeply, smoothly, and naturally. Pay attention to the inflow and outflow of your breath. Do not try to alter or control the breath. If you are distracted by thoughts floating through your mind, sounds in the surrounding environment, or sensations in the body, that's all right. Let them come and go like clouds drifting by as you bring your attention back to your breath.

Continue this process for up to twenty minutes as a beginner. You'll be able to go beyond that amount of time as you become more practiced.

....

Am I Doing This Right?

What you just read is one of the most traditional ways to meditate. Please understand that you may meditate wherever you are, at any time, and in any way you choose. However, please refrain from meditating when you're driving!

No matter where, when, why, or how you meditate, you should know that there is no wrong way to do it. If you find yourself falling asleep, that's okay. It indicates that you're tired. If you find yourself fending off a barrage of thoughts, that's okay. It indicates that you have a lot on your mind and probably need to release those thoughts before they turn into harmful stress. Let the thoughts come and go. Be the "witness" to these thoughts—don't judge them or let them influence you to act on them in any way. Acknowledge them but stay calmly detached from them. You may talk to yourself about this: "What an interesting thought. I'll think about you later. Good-bye for now." And then come back to the object of your attention—your mantra, word, or breath.

Be consistent and remember that ongoing practice brings the most profound benefits, as the mind is wily and will resist settling down at first. As for finding the right way to access the silence we have discussed, trust me. You will find it. All you need to do is show up with the intention and you will already experience an awakening to the miracle of existence. Eventually and over time your life becomes a continuous meditation, 24 hours a day, 7 days a week, 365 days a year. Yes, this *is* possible!

Meditation changes your perception of things. Your senses are enhanced in ways that are profoundly sensual. You begin to enjoy relationships, food, art, music, massage, sex, or any other pleasurable and positive experience more fully because you're more present. This is elemental in enjoying more with less, with food being a great example. If you experience the food with your senses, taking in its color, texture, and smell while chewing thoughtfully and tasting it all, you will aid digestion, feel full more quickly, lose weight, *and* experience the power of your meditation at work.

Meditation is also a prime pump for compassion. Our ability to feel greater empathy, understanding, and forgiveness, to have a nonjudgmental nature and practice loving-kindness, is tremendously enhanced. In Eastern wisdom traditions, meditation has long been a way of achieving bliss, increasing self-actualization, and exploring higher levels of consciousness. Meditation greatly enhances our inner resources for dealing creatively with challenges of any type. And we all know that we're faced with a boatload of challenges in the world in which we live today. So if you are not practicing, get with the program and begin a meditation practice here and now. Commit to this. Develop a personal statement of intent: "I intend to commune with spirit today and every day." Say it with relish and conviction. Say it out loud. Sing it if you'd like. Show yourself how serious you are. Finish reading this chapter and then put this book aside and give yourself five minutes of soul-full bliss.

If you commit to meditation, I promise you it will rock your world. It will change everything about how you experience every facet of your life. Just as with physical exercise, you will find that you do not want to compromise on your meditation time. It will become as important and integral to your day as bathing, eating, and sleeping. Coming to meditation from this perspective, you will experience its great richness in short order.

Mini-Meditations

I highly recommend setting a regular time every day for meditation, but you may also want to meditate for shorter periods during different parts of the day to carve out little pockets of peace wherever you can. These brief meditations provide chances to regroup when stress reaches hysterical peaks or energy hits unbearable lows. You may not go to your deepest, most peaceful place, but nonetheless, these can be extremely helpful times. Consider a brief two-minute breathing exercise, a walk in nature, a private moment to daydream while looking out the window, a few minutes in a serenity garden, or simply five minutes between work tasks. All are valid and viable ways to bring the benefits of meditation into your life. You will find your own path to meditation. To get started, try thinking of five simple ways to find five minutes of quiet time. Once you identify each opportunity, begin taking it. Lace short meditations throughout your day to get your breathing into balance, lower your stress level, be more alert and aware, and be a responder rather than a reactor, that knee-jerk emotional fallout from an overly stressed life.

8

breathing lessons

Breathing, then, is intercourse with the Universe, with all of life.
—JUNE SINGER

We've already experienced some healing breath practices, but here we dive deeper in. Healing breathwork is one of the most profound health and relaxation practices available to us. It begins to stabilize the nervous system within one minute. The stressors or chaos swirling around you may not go away, but proper breathing can safeguard your health and well-being even in the most challenging times. How powerful is that!

If healing breath were sold as a prescription in a bottle, it would be the best-selling drug in the world for the plethora of benefits it provides to our mind-body physiology. The most progressive integrative and functional health physicians even prescribe healing breath as their single best antistress medicine. Dr. Andrew Weil maintains, "The simplest and most powerful technique for protecting your health is breathing."

Weil teaches "breathwork"—also called diaphragmatic or belly breathing—to all his patients. "I have seen breath control alone achieve remarkable results: lowering blood pressure, ending heart arrhythmias, improving long-standing patterns of poor digestion, increasing blood circulation throughout the body, decreasing anxiety and allowing people to get off addictive antianxiety drugs and improving sleep and energy cycles," he says.

The best part about proper breathing is that we have access to its healing powers anywhere, any time. It doesn't cost anything. And there are no side effects! Only the most healthful bennies possible. To get the benefits, learn the mechanics to breathe away tension.

Breath Is Life

One wailing breath announces our arrival, just as one final breath marks our departure. In between, you breathe about 21,000 times each day, taking hundreds of millions of breaths over your lifetime. Chances are, despite these large numbers, you have not taken time to notice your breath, no less work on how to breathe.

Breath is a powerful tool that, with each inhalation, oxygenates your blood and sends it pulsing through veins throughout your body. It energizes and relaxes you simultaneously. Every exhale sends out carbon dioxide into the environment, releasing metabolic waste from your system and detoxing, purifying, and renewing your mind-body physiology.

Right now, you're breathing in some of the same air molecules as Leonard da Vinci, Sidonie-Gabrielle Colette, Buddha, William Shakespeare, or whomever else you might choose to think about. When you release a deep breath, you exhale ten sextillion air molecules, and it takes about six years for one breath to scatter across the earth's atmosphere, eventually ending up in places like

Florence, Paris, Varanasi, and London. And though you may not be able to afford to visit the Roman Forum, your breath molecules may be doing just that.

Ultimately, our breath is the life-force energy, and the way in which we mindfully breathe creates a delicious connection between the mind and the body. Whereas a disturbed and distracted mind can have a tendency to run the show, when you breathe mindfully, your mind, body, and spirit are delightfully intertwined around one another instead of being at a standoff. When we control our breath, we calm down our nervous system and create an internal rhythm that balances all our body systems and organs.

The Natural Breath

If you observe a sleeping baby, you'll witness natural, proper breathing. Watch how the little belly naturally rises and falls with each breath. This is how we are meant to breathe! Babies make full use of the diaphragm muscle in establishing a natural and oh-so-relaxing breathing rhythm.

The Mechanics of Breathing

The diaphragm muscle sandwiched between the lungs and the abdomen stretches like a drumhead across the bottom of the chest. When it contracts on the inhalation, it shortens and flattens, pushing downward on the digestive organs while lengthening the chest cavity above it. On the exhalation, the diaphragm relaxes and curves upward like a dome. The lungs do not fill or empty on their own. This expansion of the chest cavity and rib cage is what inflates and draws air into the lungs. When the chest cavity shrinks, the lungs are compressed and air is pushed out. This is the foundation of diaphragmatic breathing, or belly breathing. Many other elements come into play here—the rib cage and abdominal and back muscles along with the spine—but suffice it to say that you now know the basics to work on optimizing your breathing.

Habitual Holding Patterns That Inhibit Breathing

As we live our lives, we begin to hold life's stressors in the mind-body physiology and become tense and guarded. As a result, we unconsciously "freeze" the diaphragm, creating frequent short, shallow breaths from the upper part of the chest. This keeps us in perpetual stress mode, governed by the sympathetic nervous system. This unrelenting state of flight or flight severely degrades our bodily systems and mental processes.

Posture is also of extreme importance in breathing well. When you're curved over in a slump, with your shoulders rolling forward and with any form of forward head thrust (hello, addicted smartphone users), your chest is collapsing over your abdomen and you will have great difficulty breathing properly and exhaling stress. This is one reason we put major emphasis in yoga class on posture first (tadasana or mountain pose) and foremost as a preparation for proper breathing.

Then there's the old-school rule of "sucking in your gut," a great way to remove perceived inches from your waistline but a definite detriment to breathing.

With all of this, we tend to become shallow chest breathers. This causes us to subtly hyperventilate, with our bodily systems and mental processes suffering in the process.

Return to your beginnings and recapture diaphragmatic or belly breathing. Healing breathwork is one of the simplest and most powerful ways to decrease the stress response and increase energy levels in the mind-body physiology.

When you bring air down into the lower portion of the lungs, where the oxygen–carbon dioxide exchange is the most efficient, your mind-body physiology changes dramatically. For starters, you stop the overflow of the stress hormone cortisol through the bloodstream. You receive efficient delivery of oxygen to the brain, muscles, and organs. The movement of lymph through the lymph system is optimized, enhancing immune system functioning. Overall metabolism improves, and with it, digestive, absorptive, and eliminative processes. The heart rate slows, blood pressure normalizes, tense muscles relax, the busy mind calms down, and unhealthy emotional patterns ease up. You are shifting into the relaxation response (also called the relax and digest mode) governed by the parasympathetic nervous system.

In addition, deep breathing can relieve headaches, backaches, stomachaches, and sleeplessness. It helps normalize the body's release of the natural painkillers and mood enhancers called endorphins; boosts levels of serotonin and dopamine, the body's natural antidepressants and tranquilizers; and boosts the release of vasodilators, immunomodulators, and human growth hormone (DHEA).

Breathwork has also been shown to help those with an addiction kick the habit, whatever that addiction may be. It can help in overcoming anxiety and panic disorder. In one study, diaphragmatic breathing reduced the frequency of hot flashes in menopausal women by 50 percent.

 ## Let's Practice

Diaphragmatic/belly breathing is incredibly simple to master. Just remember to keep it soft, easy, and fluid.

For this exercise, find a quiet space where you won't be disturbed. You can stand, sit up straight, or lie down. For the most efficient flow of the life-force energy, you want your spine to be in alignment.

- Let your shoulders melt down away from your ears. Yes, just let those trapezius muscles go! Feel your rib cage and heart center opening.

- Close your eyes if you'd like. Bring in a deep breath through the nose. The nose is designed to naturally warm and filter every breath. Feel the flow of this life-giving energy as it travels into and through the length and depth of your lungs.

- You may feel the lower abdomen moving outward. Visualize every cell in your body receiving this nourishing, life-giving energy.

- As you slowly exhale (through the nostrils if possible), your abdomen will move inward. Feel the navel move inward toward the spine.

- Don't give the exhalation short shrift here. It is deeply cleansing and relaxing. Fully exhale. (Gulping in the next inhale without having fully exhaled is a primary culprit in shallow breathing.)

- Sense the release of all the stress you may be holding in any part of your body. You should begin to feel a deep sense of relaxation while at the same time sensing a heightened flow of energy.

- For those who have sinus issues, a deviated septum, asthma, or the like, do the best you can with inhaling and exhaling through the nostrils. If this is difficult, with the teeth gently together and the lips slightly open, breathe through the mouth. Keep this process soft and not strained.

- Take ten deep diaphragmatic breaths as outlined above. Work toward full breathing that is deep, soft, and easy, with no pauses or jerking movements. The deeper and easier the breath is, the more the torso expands and contracts. You are in essence creating a wavelike massaging action on the 60 trillion cells in your body. With regular practice, this type of breathing can become an everyday habit, not just an exercise to be performed at a set time.

- Watching the gentle inflow and outflow of the breath is one of simplest and most beautiful ways to meditate, accessible to virtually everyone.

- You can heighten the experience by prolonging each inhalation and exhalation or by increasing the length of the overall breathwork session. Breathwork is an integral part of meditation and yoga as well as visualization, so if you plan to build any of these techniques into your life, be sure to master breathing first.

....

Got Prana?

Diaphragmatic breathing is a foundational technique in pranayama. In Ayurveda/yoga practice, *pranayama* is Sanskrit for "the science of breath." Prana is the life-force energy. When we practice any form of pranayama, we are mastering the life-force energy in and around us. When prana flows freely through the 75,000 energy circuits throughout the mind-body physiology (nadis in Ayurveda, meridians in traditional Chinese medicine), we raise our vibration and feel vitalized and healthy. Conversely, when prana is blocked, fatigue, *dis*-ease, and illness may follow. You may choose to increase your repertoire of breathing capabilities well beyond the foundational approach. The techniques are incredibly numerous and varied: some soothing, some cooling, some stimulating. There are also breath retention techniques that can greatly affect one's level of energy or relaxation (for those who are uninitiated in pranayama, guidance with a teacher is recommended for breath retention techniques). All offer great rewards for your future exploration.

Breathe Retention 101

The pranayama technique *Kumbhaka* entails focusing on a pause at the top of the inhalation and/or the bottom of the exhalation. This is done to a certain pattern or ratio. You may choose to consciously lengthen and hold at the top of the inhalation to increase your energy level, whereas lengthening and holding at the bottom of the exhalation enhances the relaxation response. Let's look at some examples.

Let's Practice

Here are the basics for practicing breath retention. The pattern for each is inhale, hold, exhale, hold, repeat.

Relaxing effect:

- Inhale for a count of four or six through your nose until your lungs are completely full.

- Hold at the top for a count of one.

- Exhale through the nose for eight—taking all eight counts to release the breath. Concentrate on a slowed down, controlled release of the breath.

- When the lungs are completely empty, hold for a count of four.

- Repeat for several breaths or even several minutes.

- Adjust the counts to be faster or slower, depending on your lung capacity.

This practice is great at any time and especially before meditation to center yourself. You may also choose to use this breathing pattern during any "mindfulness in motion" activity such as yoga or tai chi.

Balanced effect:

- Inhale for a count of six through your nose until your lungs are completely full.

- Hold at the top for a count of either one or two.

- Exhale through the nose for six.

- When the lungs are completely empty, hold for a count of either one or two.

- Repeat for several breaths or even several minutes.

Energizing effect:

- Inhale for a count of six through your nose until your lungs are completely full.

- Hold at the top for a count of four.

- Exhale through the nose for six.

- When the lungs are completely empty, hold for a count of one.

- Repeat for several breaths or even several minutes.

Again, in yoga we generally recommend instruction on breath retention by a qualified teacher. And there are contraindications such as untreated heart disease and pregnancy, among others. So even though this is generally regarded as safe, use caution with these basic techniques.

But let me leave you with this: Aside from all the mind-body health benefits that we've discussed, deep, gentle breathing is one of the most effortless highs that you'll ever experience. Try it right now and often. There are few things in life as satisfying as this gentle dive into tranquility.

....

Breath Check

Rest one hand on your chest and one on your belly. Inhale and exhale several times. Have your hands moved? They should! You want your abdomen to rise like a dome as you pull in a deep breath. As you exhale, your belly will deflate and return to its resting position. This is diaphragmatic breathing.

Don't get too caught up in the rise and fall of your stomach. Focus on smooth, effortless inhales and exhales, making sure your belly rises and falls. Incredibly simple and powerful, diaphragmatic breathing decreases our stress response and increases body energy and alertness of mind.

9

emotional housecleaning

Despite how open, peaceful, and loving you attempt to be, people can only meet you, as deeply as they've met themselves. This is the heart of clarity.
—MATT KAHN

Each of us makes his own weather, determines the color of the skies in the emotional universe which he inhabits.
—FULTON J. SHEEN

Our issues truly are in our tissues. Unprocessed emotions get stuck within us. It's important to feel all the emotions that bubble up inside us, but it's also important to know when to let go instead of stuffing it. If you stuff, it just keeps coming up at times and in ways that can keep you from being your joyous self. This becomes so toxic to our mind-body physiology, these unprocessed emotions. Our emotions are at the root (squared!) of so much of our stress and discomfort. They tie into our relationships as well as our communication style. When you learn how to change your perception of or emotional attitude toward stressful situations, you remove their ability to negatively affect you. Regular emotional housecleanings are warranted in our self-care regimen. Acceptance and forgiveness are elemental in this process as well.

Emotional Rescue

In his song "Emotional Weather Report," Tom Waits predicts "tornado watches issued shortly before noon Sunday for the areas including the western region of my mental health and the northern portion of my ability to deal rationally with my disconcerted precarious emotional situation. It's cold out there."

Weather is a particularly apt metaphor for emotions. Blistering heat, frigid cold, drought, calm waters, clear skies, radiant sunshine—all are forces of powerful energy, just as the experiences of our lives, our past and present relationships, become part of us, down to the cellular level.

In the old comic strip *Li'l Abner*, there was a character who walked around with his own personal storm system roiling overhead. We've all known people who move moodily through their day, raining on many a parade. Others go beyond simple negativity to place their emotional outbursts front and center; still others sink into grief, despair, and fear. Often these emotional challenges can have genetic components or may result from chemical/hormonal imbalances. They can even be set off by environmental triggers. These people may require special help to negotiate their way out of their emotional prison.

Yet for most of us, negative flare-ups are more immediate, triggered by our day-to-day experiences. This everyday play of emotion has the potential to be one of the most predominant stressors in our lives and can be a source of tremendous toxicity, wreaking all manner of misery and mayhem on our lives, including failed relationships, addictions, and potentially serious health issues.

Because we all differ in our life experiences, what evokes a strong emotional response will differ among us also. Developing the emotional intelligence to handle the ebb and flow of feeling is therefore a different process for everyone.

But developing the discipline to manage the way we respond to changes and challenges in our lives is not only possible, it's life-giving. As we learn to observe and respond to our emotions with grace, empathy, and maturity, our mindfulness rewires our neurological system and harmonizes our brain wave patterns so that it becomes easier to respond in the future.

The stakes are high. If we indirectly deal with our emotions, stifle them, or vacillate, we live indirectly and thereby cheat ourselves of transformation. Have you ever dealt with an adult and thought, "He reacts like my teenage son!" In fact, adults can be "stopped" at certain ages in their emotional development and remain there if they do not take action. When we divert or block our pain, conflict, or fear, we become anesthetized to life and truly narrow our consciousness. Our senses become dulled, along with our capacity for intimacy with self and others.

Housecleaning

All of us tend to walk through life carrying a lot of baggage: past hurts, resentments, and sadness. It is important to let these unhealthy emotions go before they create fragmentation within us, leaving us confused and depleted.

The skill of "present moment awareness" is invaluable for leaving the past and exuberantly enjoying the present. This skill gives you the ability to place your attention on your emotions from the moment you get up in the morning till the time you go to bed at night. It's a conscious witnessing of behaviors, moods, and actions.

Key to present moment awareness is *not* to avoid an emotion but to attend to it, to feel it, to sense it without trying to analyze, change, or end it. Let your emotions be and let them speak to you. When you've done this successfully, you can let go and surrender to the flow of the emotion toward healing and balance.

Knowing your emotional landscape in this way will prepare you to take to take full responsibility for your own feelings. This in turn will allow you to inform rather than blame when you communicate your needs to others.

Practicing Housecleaning

Here's a practice that can help you work through an emotion from your past. You can also use these techniques to help deal immediately with a highly charged emotional encounter.

1. Identify an experience that has provoked an uncomfortable or toxic emotion. Do this in a very matter-of-fact way.

2. State the reasons for this emotion (the event or issue) to yourself or out loud or write them down as clearly as possible. Try not to be accusatory in tone or use words that reinforce a sense of victimization but be as accurate as possible.

3. Focus on the emotion. Emotions are thoughts connected to sensations in the body. That's why they're called feelings. Allow the feeling or "aura" of the emotion to well up and fully witness it in mind and body.

4. Catalog the physical sensations that this emotion creates, identifying the location and intensity of the feelings. Does the emotion create a backache, stomachache, or headache? Does it make your heart race? Be very specific.

5. Identify the beliefs that support the feelings you're having. For instance, if you're angry at a sibling for always using your cosmetics without asking, the supporting belief that brings on the anger may be "I can't afford to be supporting her product usage and mine." When you identify the belief in this way, you can work toward a resolution by communicating with the other person. Instead of lashing out in anger, you are maturely coming from a supported belief.

6. Really reflect on what the emotion reveals about you: a fearful ego, a need for approval, a need for control, a need for respect, a need for love? Try to be very clear on what it is that you feel you need, that you may not be getting. This is where regular meditation, as we've discussed in previous chapters, becomes a very valuable practice. You're more connected to your inner voice, to your higher self.

7. Now work toward releasing the emotion and any painful body sensations. Have this intention: "I will let go of this anger toward my sister." Affirm it. Perhaps build a ritual around this: free-form ecstatic dance, energetic breathing—anything that helps discharge the emotion from your mind-body physiology. This very conscious act prevents the negative emotion from controlling you any longer.

Although steps 8 and 9 are optional, try them; even if you don't, do step 10:

8. Reframe the way you see the situation. See the opportunities along with the risks in difficult emotional situations. For instance, an argument may give you the opportunity to practice empathy as you strengthen your listening skills. You may begin to understand relationships better.

9. In crisis situations, when someone else is forcefully pushing his or her ideas onto you or attacking you or your beliefs, try this instead of fighting back: Sidestep and deflect the force of the attack, using your energy to find a middle ground where the problem at hand is addressed. Avoid making statements; instead, ask questions while inviting advice and constructive criticism. A solution to the problem may be revealed. Lighten the mood with a joke or a smile. In any case, you will become an effective negotiator, an important skill in both our personal and our professional lives.

10. Now that you have released the emotion that you're working with, celebrate! Take a luxurious bath. Go somewhere beautiful for a walk. Prepare and eat a nourishing meal. Listen to your favorite music. Get a massage.

When you have finished the entire process, tune in to your body and mind. Do you notice a shift in attitude? Congratulations! You just gave yourself a tremendous gift.

....

EI

Emotional intelligence (EI) is a trait many beauty professionals possess in high levels. It is what makes us "people people," but it also makes us prone to hurts and resentments. Use these five skills to get the most out of EI.

- **Self-awareness**—Place attention on your emotions, recognizing feelings as they occur and discriminating between them.

- **Mood management**—Live an emotional life without being anesthetized or hijacked by it. Avoid being paralyzed by depression or worry or swept away by anger. Let feelings move through you but don't let anything negative take hold.

- **Self-motivation**—Persist in channeling your impulses in pursuit of your goal. This builds resiliency. Even if the going is difficult, you will be able to move through it and proceed with your intentions, your peace, and your life.

- **Empathy**—Recognize feelings in others and tune in to their verbal and nonverbal cues. Walk in their shoes. Everything will become better around you if you understand others and their needs.

- **Management of relationships**—Handle feelings in relationships with commitment, honesty, and an open heart to move toward negotiation, resolution of conflict, and harmony. Discuss conflict without rancor. Diplomacy is a powerful tool for an enlightened mind.

Emotional Physics

Many of us laid down emotional roots at a point early in our lives when we experienced abuse. Early conditioning toward physical, verbal, or emotional abuse, if not processed fully, can take a tremendous toll on health.

Those suffering from these kinds of destructive emotions can benefit greatly both mentally and physically by some manner of therapeutic intervention. Dr. John E. Sarno, professor of Clinical Rehabilitation Medicine at the New York University School of Medicine, draws a direct connection between repressed emotion and illness in two books: *Healing Back Pain* **and** *The Mindbody Prescription: Healing the Body, Healing the Pain*.

Similarly, neuroscientist Candace Pert in her *Molecules of Emotion* makes the case that every thought we have creates a molecule in our bodies. If we have angry thoughts, we create angry cells; sad thoughts, "sad" cells; happy thoughts, "happy" cells. Her provocative argument calls on us to heal ourselves by modulating our emotional responses.

I once met a woman who had been an abused child and who as an adult had debilitating rheumatoid arthritis for almost twenty years. With caring help, she got in touch with her anger and resentment and began to forgive her father. As she connected with her spirit and healed her mind and emotions, her body began the work of healing itself as well. Today she is prescription drug- and pain-free.

She found the way out of her emotional prison, as anyone can. If you are facing significant struggles with your emotions, seek out a trusted friend who will listen without judgment, a spiritual counselor, or a trained professional. Learn to care for your emotional life and you will learn to care for your physical needs. The two are wrapped as tightly as, say, body and soul.

If you think about it, examples are everywhere. Another woman—a writer—suddenly experienced terrific pain in her lower back and tried countless remedies. She sought out many different forms of relief from Western medical treatments and Eastern healing techniques, such as acupuncture. She found a little relief in each, but always returned to the same levels of pain. After years on this merry-go-round, a healer suggested her physical pain was attached to a fear that she hadn't overcome. Indeed, it was attached to her checkbook. She slowly worked through, in her rational mind, her fear about the possibility of going broke or being without a home or food. The pain left and now, when she feels it knocking, she addresses fear instead of reaching for the pain relief.

That's right: You are a single organism and what you think and how you feel have an effect on your physical health, just as your physical health impacts what you think and how you feel. Taking care of yourself includes understanding your emotions.

10

setting healthy boundaries

When we fail to set boundaries and hold people accountable,
we feel used and mistreated. This is why we sometimes attack who they are,
which is far more hurtful than addressing a behavior or a choice
— BRENE BROWN

"No" is a complete sentence.
— ANNE LAMOTT

Setting healthy boundaries is the perfect accompaniment to emotional housecleaning. Have you ever been a doormat for someone's negativity or been railroaded into doing something that didn't feel right or safe? Do "energy vampires" float in and out of your life, draining every ounce of your life-force energy? What do these situations have in common? The answer is undefined, weak, or nonexistent boundaries that can make us feel like a victim. Setting healthy safe boundaries is an important part of our self-care, deserving of our attention and intention. It's also an integral life skill in any relationship, especially in situations in which people are controlling, aren't accountable, or won't take responsibility for their actions. It is, however, our duty to take responsibility for the way we allow others to treat us.

Setting Healthy Boundaries

We need to be able to tell other people when they are acting in ways that are not acceptable to us. Many of us remain quiet because we fear conflict or rejection. We also do not express our needs, make requests, ask for support, put forth an alternative point of view, or share our truth for the same reasons. Practice can help us take responsibility for our needs and our "truth" and then express them. It's all in how you consciously communicate.

Boundary setting is the practice of communicating *and* asserting your personal values and needs to prevent having them compromised or violated. It's learning how to negotiate having your needs met as well as how to say no rather than being manipulated into doing anything you do not want to do. Finally, clear, strong boundaries are healthy for your mind, body, and spirit. Allowing anyone to violate what is life-affirming for you drains the joy from your life.

Remember, we condition people how to treat us by what we allow, stop, or reinforce.

Our physical and emotional health is at stake when we fail to say no to excessive demands or abusive behavior, whether subtle or blatant. Any relationship in which we feel a diminished sense of self makes it difficult for us to have our needs met. When we constantly give to others at the expense of fulfilling our own needs or dreams, not only do we feel drained, we can feel hurt, angry, resentful, and even hopeless. Why would we want to put ourselves in this position? Boundary setting allows us to stand in our power and be treated with the respect we deserve.

Boundary setting is a necessary step in learning how to love and be a friend to ourselves. These imaginary lines we establish around ourselves help define limits and protect the mind, heart, and soul from the unhealthy, draining, and damaging behavior of others. It allows us to be at our best and feel great about ourselves. Setting boundaries frees up tremendous positive energy that we can devote to self-actualization (achieving our full human potential) while serving humanity and the greater good.

This, my friends, is what "fulfilling our dharma" looks like.

Where to Begin

First, become aware of how you feel when you're with someone. If you don't feel comfortable, safe, or good about yourself in a person's presence, important boundaries are being violated. It is important not to explain or reason your feelings away here. If you feel it, it exists.

As a general exercise, you may want to think of and then write down a list of at least a dozen behaviors or things that people may no longer say or do to you in your presence. This list can range from"I don't like it when he snaps his gum in my ear" to "no more lies." This list is an important guide to honor and care for your spirit for all of life.

Define Your Needs

You need to be quite clear on what your needs are in order to define boundaries. (Don't be wishy-washy here!) Also, remember that boundaries will shift and change according to the rhythm of our lives. A daily mindfulness practice allows for clarity and flexibility in navigating life's changes; thus, any boundaries that need to be refined or redefined can be. As individuals change, so do boundaries.

Beyond physiological needs (hunger, thirst, sleep, shelter), fundamental human needs include attention, affection, appreciation, and acceptance. These needs can be expressed in a number of ways.

Our emotions (both comfortable and otherwise) derive from needs. When we perceive that our physical and psychological needs are met, we feel comfort, pleasure, and happiness. When we perceive that our physical and psychological needs are not met, we feel distress, pain, and sadness. When pain-based or unmet needs are stored rather than resolved, it often leads to anxiety, hostility, guilt, and eventually depression. Contemplate and define what needs are not being met in your important relationships. Once they are identified, you can not only strive to have your needs met but also resolve any stressful emotions.

Conscious Communication

Setting boundaries requires clear, compassionate communication as you inform, educate, and request of others what you require. You need to feel heard, appreciated, empowered, respected, and

Meditation for a Most Basic Need: A Good Sleep

Meditation stimulates the pineal gland, a part of the endocrine system nestled deep within the brain, an important regulator for maintaining health. The pineal gland is a major control center for the production of hormones that regulate body function. One of these, melatonin, helps induce sleep, among other functions. Simply put, more melatonin means better sleep. Less melatonin means less sleep. As we age, we make less melatonin and have greater difficulty sleeping. Stress also decreases the production of melatonin.

Meditation can increase melatonin production by reducing stress and stimulating the pineal gland. The more you practice meditation, the greater is the production of melatonin and the better your quality of sleep. Then there is melatonin's effect in fighting cancer. Melatonin has been shown to inhibit the growth of certain cancer cells. It also binds to white blood cells, stimulating the release of cancer-fighting compounds called interleukins and interferon. In some studies, the one-year survival rate of patients treated with chemotherapy and melatonin versus chemotherapy alone was significantly higher. Those treated with melatonin also had fewer side effects from the chemotherapy. That is one more provocative reason Eastern holistic techniques such as meditation should be part of cancer protocols in traditional Western medicine.

safe. Translate your thoughts into honest but nonconfrontational language that is devoid of blame. Speak from a place of kindness and humility.

Remember, you are setting boundaries as a way to love yourself, not as a way to vent or rage against others. It is best to proceed when you are calm and very clear about what you'll allow or not allow a person to do in your presence. If communication is an issue for you, you may want to consider studying Marshall Rosenberg's Nonviolent Communication (NVC) model (www.nonviolentcommunication.com and www.cnvc.org). This is the model we utilize in the Emotional Enfoldment module of the Chopra Center's Ayurveda program.

You want to avoid words that put the person you're speaking with on the defensive and encourage victimization ("You betrayed me," "You manipulated me," "You patronized me"). Ideally, the words you use express your feelings *and* unmet needs in a safe, nonthreatening way ("I feel afraid," "I feel helpless," "I feel overwhelmed," "I don't want to feel this way any longer").

It is important to state our feelings out loud and to precede the feeling with "I feel." (When we say, "I am angry, I'm hurt," we are stating that the feeling is who we are. We are not our emotions. They are but one part of our being, not us in our totality.) This is owning the feeling. It is important to do this for ourselves. By stating the feeling out loud we are affirming that we have a right to feelings. We are affirming it to ourselves and taking responsibility for owning our reality. It is vitally important to own our own voices, to own our right to speak up for ourselves.

Communicate your need as clearly as possible while defining the behavior that you find unacceptable. Here are some examples:

"You're very hostile" (this is a judgment) versus "I feel threatened (or unsafe) when you use such a hostile tone of voice. I cannot feel threatened. I need to feel safe" (this gets to the point of what triggered your concerns).

"You're always so sarcastic" versus "I feel like I'm not being taken seriously. I dislike your sarcastic tone when I'm talking about something that is important to me."

Do you see the difference?

Remember, when you claim your boundaries, you're not defining, attacking, or judging someone as a person. Rather, you are defining a behavior that needs to change for you to feel comfortable. This is the boundary.

Granted, when things escalate, defining boundaries may need to be more forceful or you may need to remove yourself from the situation: "In this moment, I find your behavior unacceptable. If you wish to discuss this later, I'm open to that. But for now, I feel we need a pause, a breathing space between us, so I'm leaving."

You may even need to remove certain individuals from your life altogether. When you create new, healthy boundaries that honor your needs and help you affirm your power, you are taking care of yourself, your intentions, and your dreams. If there are people who then unrelentingly test every boundary you have, let them go. This *does not apply to your children*—or anyone else's for that matter. Boundary busting is their job as they explore the world. But the adults who relentlessly push and take and leave you wanting? Radically let go of those who do not have your needs and deep nourishment in mind.

You don't have to do anything: Just withdraw. Or you can state your reasons clearly and logically and then withdraw. The important point is that you remove this source of discomfort in your life and move forward, becoming your best self.

Next Steps

When you inform others of your boundaries, you can expect some resistance. Some (especially children) may test you until they realize that you mean business and that their unacceptable words or behaviors will no longer be tolerated. Make certain there are set consequences when boundaries are violated.

With consistency, our boundaries become automatic. People will become respectful without your having to tell them to. A lovely bonus of setting boundaries is that as you set them, others learn to do this for themselves. As you honor yourself and your needs, you become a role model and teach others to become more respectful of themselves and others.

In the end, this is about positive, life-affirming energy. When we have clear boundaries, we attract similar energy into our lives; we attract those who have clear boundaries, self-respect, and in turn respect for others.

In conclusion, insist that your boundaries are always honored. Express gratitude to those who respect your boundaries. And remember the golden rule: Respect and honor others' boundaries as you would have them respect and honor yours.

11

become a physical activist

You have to stay in shape. My grandmother, she started walking five miles a day when she was 60. She's 97 today and we don't know where the hell she is.
—ELLEN DEGENERES

As you walk, cultivate a sense of ease. There's no hurry to get anywhere, no destination to reach. You're just walking. This is a good instruction: just walk. As you walk, as you let go of the desire to get somewhere, you begin to sense the joy in simply walking, in being in the present moment. Walks are like snowflakes: No two are the same. Swing your arms, swivel your hips. Take long steps and then short ones. Feel the difference. Look around and smell the air. That is always changing too. You begin to comprehend the preciousness of each step. It's an extraordinarily precious experience to walk on this earth.

Our bodies love to move! Every minute we devote to physical activity is a blessing for the body, mind, and soul. Along with proper nutrition, it's one of the greatest healers. Movement is an incredible stress buster. It raises serotonin levels in the body (remember, serotonin is the body's natural "feel-good" chemical).

Yet so many choose not to engage in the most minimal amount of daily activity necessary for health. (More than a third of all Americans say they do not move in their leisure time at all!) This is where sweet mindfulness comes into play yet again. When we see our mindfulness in motion activities as play, we approach with a mind-set that embraces the benefits that cardio work, strengthening, and flexibility afford us and our health, longevity, moods, and energy levels.

Mindfulness in Motion

We all know how regular physical activity is essential for our well-being. Right? Yet even though it is one of the foremost critical ingredients for living a vibrant, healthy, balanced life, many place it at the bottom of their priority list. My friends, this is where sweet mindfulness comes into play again. Spirit loves to play! I know how good my daily play makes me feel in body, mind, and mood. Why not see all our daily movement activities as play? This shift in perception can be the spark that changes *everything*.

Mindfulness Is Key

Long the bastion of meditative, internally focused physical activities such as yoga, tai chi, and qigong (chi kung), mindfulness practice is quickly becoming *the* remedy for increasing our enjoyment of any physical activity or exercise. Remember, mindfulness

Each Journey Begins
with a Single Step

Perhaps we should all rethink how we define movement in our lives. Walking is exercise, and your body loves it! Most people shoot for at least 10,000 steps a day, all easily tracked on a smartphone. Walking from the car to the store counts. Those stairs between floors at work count. If you are engaged in movement now, start counting steps. Get to your goal and then jump off and try some aerobics such as biking and jogging. Walk for thirty seconds and then jog for thirty seconds as part of a thirty-minute routine. This is known as interval training, and it is great for the heart and has many variations. Take a yoga class. Buy an app for your phone that shows strength training movements. Before you invest in hand weights, fill up a couple of soda bottles, cap them, and use them as weights. Bend and stretch while in the yard or gardening. Housework counts. When you dust, really reach for the highest spot, feeling your muscles stretch and work. Start slowly. If you pull your muscles on the first day, you won't want to continue. Be aware of the movement in your life and how it feels. Build on that.

means paying attention to the present moment in a way that notices thoughts, sensations, or feelings in a compassionate and nonjudgmental way.

If you're having trouble sticking with a fitness routine, instead of letting your mind drift into the ether when you're working out, pay attention. Don't pound the equipment, making lists in your head. Pay attention to every nuance of how and what your body feels in a nonjudgmental way and you'll derive greater satisfaction from your morning walk, circuit training, bicycling, swimming, or whatever else you do.

Mindfulness is the number one remedy to help us develop a lifelong fitness mind-set for a healthier life. Instead of thinking, "Exercise isn't my thing" or "I'll be miserable," mindfulness allows you to focus on how your body enjoys breathing and moving. It gets you out of your head and builds awareness of how your amazing, miraculous body expresses itself through movement. When physical activity becomes meditation in motion, every movement and every breath is infused with a sense of playfulness and joy.

These assertions have been confirmed by research studies that show that those who incorporate mindfulness into their fitness regimens feel better about exercising, are more satisfied with their routines, and tend to exercise more consistently and frequently.

If you're churning out a few miles on the treadmill, notice the rhythm of your pulse, each full inhalation and exhalation, each leg striding, each foot landing. If you're doing a set of bench presses, notice the bar path, focus on feeling your chest muscles contract at the top of each rep, notice the strain of the weight through your pectorals, and feel the controlled belly breathing along with core tension. Pay exquisite attention to every facet of movement and you not only enjoy the activity more fully, you experience a profound connection with this amazing body of yours, the earthly vessel for spirit.

Studies show how mindfulness practice enhances positive emotion: The human brain likes to focus on one thing at a time. (You can see how modern life pulled the brain out of its comfort zone.) Instead of mental chatter that focuses on what we don't like, we home in on the essence of our experience, noticing the bare sensations, the feeling of movement, blood flow, internal heat, and more. The mind thrives when focused, and that thriving affects the entire mind-body physiology. We're happier, we experience life more deeply, and we are open to what the future may bring.

Mindfulness stops negative thought processes that persuade people to skip exercising. If you're someone who lacks motivation to exercise, you back it up with mental chatter such as "It's cold out," "I'm too tired," "I hate exercising," "I'm terrible at it," or "What's the use?" When you take note of those mental barriers and acknowledge them without giving in to them, you can move past them to make a different choice. In the process of making a different choice, you change the way you feel about yourself. You've essentially given yourself an upvote, a reason to feel stronger in your choices, not weaker or less engaged.

Mindfulness allows you to notice the inner thoughts that can sabotage your efforts and prevents you from being ruled by them. When you are mindful, you notice any self-doubt and are able to unhook from that line of thinking and drop into your body. You notice the thoughts and see that they're temporary. The thought passes, the sensations change, and you enter more fully into the present moment, connecting with your beautiful body in motion.

Mindfulness helps us cultivate an entirely new idea of what exercise should be. We can get stuck on notions of what exercise looks or feels like (for example, daily trips to the gym to do intense cardio or lift clattering weights). Our limited perceptions can cause us to give up. A mindful take on exercise, however, can liberate us from our rather limited ideas about it. When we change our perception of what exercise should look like, it frees us to experiment and explore different options that work specifically for us.

A key part of a mindfulness approach to fitness is acknowledging that we will probably drift away from it just the way our attention drifts away from focusing on a mantra or our breath during meditation. By seeing any and all physical activity as a mindfulness practice, we know that we'll drift from our practice and miss some workouts. Therefore, when we drift from our daily or weekly goals, we should adopt an attitude of compassion for ourselves and simply keep coming back to our intention over and over. In meditation, there is a constant letting go of distractions and we keep coming back to our mantra or breath. So too in our fitness regimen. We compassionately let go of any self-judgment for any lapses in our exercise routine and just keep coming back again and again to our genuine intention to keep exercising regularly. Paying attention to our peccadilloes and coming back to our self-care intentions can be transferred to any and all daily activities in our life.

Healing Movement

Our bodies love to move! They're meant to move. Every second we devote to physical activity is a blessing for the body, mind, and soul. It's simply vital to our well-being. Aside from antibiotics for a life-threatening infection, there's no medicine any doctor can prescribe that can affect our longevity and quality of life like regular exercise. Along with proper nutrition it's one of the greatest healers. It benefits *every* body system (the circulatory, respiratory, digestive, excretory, nervous, endocrine, immune, integumentary, skeletal, muscular, and reproductive systems). It's an incredible stress buster, improves sleep, boosts mood (gets those wonderful feel-good chemicals flowing: endorphins, serotonin, and dopamine), and assists in detoxification. It is one of the most powerful beautifiers available to us, creating both inner *and* outer beauty. The more efficiently our nutrient rich blood circulates, the more beautiful (and healthy) our skin, hair, nails, and eyes will be.

Healing movement can be any form of physical activity. The National Institutes of Health designates that key aspects of physical fitness include a well-rounded program of cardio, weight-bearing, and flexibility exercises or activities. Try to include all three in your daily fitness regimen. Physical activity such as yoga, Pilates, tai chi, and qigong encourage a balance between the mental and physical, as do long delicious walks, dancing, swimming, gardening, and the like. These are all opportunities to slow down and be mindful of the moment. Any physical activity can become a meditation if you direct your attention to that intention and keep it there throughout the activity.

continues on page 156

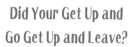

Did Your Get Up and
Go Get Up and Leave?

According to the surgeon general, only 26 percent of the U.S. population exercises regularly. This is woeful! In a society so sedentary, none of these facts is surprising:

* Large numbers of us feel spiritually deprived. When we are disconnected from our source or spirit, lethargy and inertia can set in. A spirit is imbued with energy, and if you have none, you cannot thrive. You were engineered to move—the human body does it brilliantly—and therefore, you should move. Besides, the more you do, the more you *can* do, and the intention is to keep engaging deeply with life.

* Depression is more prevalent than ever, with an estimated 20 million-plus Americans experiencing some form of it. According to the World Health Organization, more than 350 million people worldwide suffer from depression. It is a leading cause of disability and lost productivity, and we are all aware of what that does to the human spirit. That vicious circle of negative feeling turning to lethargy and then becoming more negativity turns into an insidious depression that can and does kill.

* One-third of the American population is obese, and at least 20 percent of individuals in this country are over their acceptable weight. This remains true despite the fat figure of $40 billion a year being

poured into everything and anything connected to weight loss. Get off this teeter-totter if you're on it. Stop fad dieting. Eat whole foods that nourish. Move. Do not obsess about how you look. Keep to your intentions.

* The rise in childhood obesity (and consequently adult-onset diabetes in children) is tracking upward at an alarming pace. Children take cues from adults, and the less movement they see, the less they engage in. Since adults provide the food as well, kids can become nutritional victims to their parents' busy schedules or love of processed snacks. Move and play with children. Feed them the same whole, nourishing foods that you eat. Or if the running shoe is on the other foot, let children draw you into their play and fitness. Movement is a great way—like meals—for a family to come together, talk, laugh, and enjoy life.

Are all these facts manifestations of a crisis in consciousness? Why is it that so many of us forfeit health and happiness and instead choose a love affair with the couch and TV? Are we so anesthetized to life? How could such a collectively intelligent population as ours become so fat and out of shape? This epidemic even has a name: *sedentary death syndrome*. Yes, it's true! Frank W. Booth, a professor at the University of Missouri–Columbia, coined the term to lend this chronic and potentially fatal condition credibility and perhaps make our government pay more attention and devote more funding to getting America back on its feet.

I truly wish I had the persuasive power or the eloquence to convince everyone I meet of the importance of moving our bodies abundantly. Yet on the whole, as a society we have become averse to "getting a move on." This is reflected in our skyrocketing health care problems and costs. We dramatically benefit from our physicality and our energy levels by conditioning our bodies for the activity and work that we demand of them every day. We should appreciate the joy of how a strong, fit, and healthy body feels. It is exhilarating! As your muscles make themselves known, you'll feel a sense of accomplishment and self-reliance. You can *do* more. No doubt, physical activity has tremendous healing powers and restorative effects. The best part is that you can begin this process of getting physical where you are today and steadily progress toward your own optimal fitness whatever your age, weight, gender, or current condition. Just like Ellen's grandma!

Just Do It!

As with any life-affirming practice, the key is to psyche ourselves to, as Nike says, "just do it." Many of us look for the inspiration to become active. It's so much easier to become the sloth or couch potato in a convenience-oriented world where all manner of technology in the form of remote controls, leaf blowers, and drive-up windows has streamlined our lives while rendering our bodies more static and immobile. In addition, worksite and metropolitan areas have been designed to minimize walking while increasing commercial convenience. Why, we've engineered movement right out of our lives! (Please park at the absolute outer edge of the parking lot and walk. And use the stairs instead of the escalator whenever possible.) Please rethink all the movements you make during the day and try to use the more physical approach whenever possible. In a sociocultural sense, we have really stacked the deck against becoming devotees of consistent daily exercise. But I have faith in your ingenuity. Get around all the convenience and give your life some elbow grease. Walk to the store or ride a bike. Park as far as you can from the door and walk. Use the stairs. We must simply set this as a powerful daily intention and not back away from it. Our lives might just depend on it. Remember that energy follows intention.

As Dr. Gerald Fletcher of the American Heart Association says, "The problem is that people don't understand the importance of exercise until they are lying in the cardiac care unit. Too many just want to sit and watch TV and take pills for their heart disease. Well, there's no exercise pill. People just have to do it."

Don't let a catastrophic illness be what it takes for you to become physically active. Perhaps we can reframe our way of thinking about physical activity, treating it as a lifelong prescription for health and longevity. Perhaps along with your devoted mindfulness, your intention, and your sense of playfulness, the following section of this chapter may help you break through any barriers to becoming a fiercely devoted physical activist.

Five Easy Pieces

America's great wit, Mark Twain, once famously said "Oh, I get the urge to exercise every now and then, but I just lay down and it goes away." Funny, yes, but physical movement is far more entertaining.

continues on page 160

Let's Get Physical

Movement falls into three categories: cardiovascular, flexibility, and strength training. Do some of each when you exercise, to create a balance. All the while, focus on what you are doing, staying mindful of breath and sensation. Listen to your body carefully. How does it feel? Does it love one movement and not another? Why? As you build muscle and endurance, you'll also build a greater understanding of your own strengths, inside and out.

Cardiovascular—or aerobic—movement strengthens the body's ability to pump blood and oxygen to all parts of the body, even those parts you sit on (hopefully not for too many hours a day!) Simply put, cardiovascular workouts strengthen the heart. These activities include walking, biking, jogging, running, jumping rope, hiking, dancing, power yoga, Pilates, and swimming. You can build your cardiovascular health by parking your car at the far end of the lot and walking to the building, by taking the stairs, and by taking a walk at lunch. Make your intention to add this kind of movement into your daily life and you'll be surprised at how many forward steps you take. (Try one of the step-counting apps on your Smart phone.)

Flexibility is easiest understood by watching a cat wake from a nap. She rises, stretches her front legs, arches her body, and stretches it out as far as it will go. In humans, this movement releases body tissue tension and stretches out tendons, ligaments, muscles, connective tissue (fascia), and even veins and arteries (both become brittle if not stretched inside the body.) As you stretch, turn your focus to your breath, and you will meet your highest vibration or energy source. This is what happens in yoga, tai chi, Pilates, dance, and Nia.

Strength training or weight-bearing movement is not just for Arnold Schwarzenegger, nor will it give you muscles like his. What it does do is build your power, endurance, balance, and coordination. Lifting weights reduces cellulite, burns fat, builds bone, and adds muscle, and, therefore, definition, to your body. It also develops balance, something key in preventing falls as you age. Lift free weights. Either invest in hand weights or lift cans or bottles, increasing the weight incrementally. (Fill a bottle with water, one of the weightiest things around.) Work out on the machines at a gym or use resistance bands—a small investment—at home. Some strengthening exercises use your own body as the weight; these include walking, jogging, running, yoga, and Pilates.

Bodies were made to move and the more you move yours, the more you'll want to move. The saying "a body in motion tends to stay in motion" is true.

Movement will transform your health and your life. Here are five easy steps to get going:

Change Your Mind-Set

A reason not to exercise—the viewpoint that it's "work"—is the reason many people fail to use movement to access spirit in their lives. They feel movement is somehow unpleasant and not an important part of life. How untrue! If they experienced the opening of the body's pathways after movement and a deep, peaceful mind, they'd change their attitude. Movement would become something they really want to do instead of something they have to do.

Get in contact with your body—how it looks and feels as you move. When you move, your sweat releases toxins, stress levels drop, your blood pumps, and your brain clears. That, many say, is the reason they exercise in the first place—that end of the workout bliss. Set your intentions on daily exercise and put energy into it. If you have become complacent about your body, spend time around someone who can no longer use theirs. I've worked with many a stroke victim and wheelchair-bound patient, and they are a reminder of how fragile we are. Spending time with such a person will really change your point of view.

Find Time for Movement

Difficulty finding time is perhaps the most frequent reason folks cite for not working out. It is a biggie for many, but can be overcome. And you don't have to hit the gym at 5 am and be out by 7 and on the road by 8. In fact, you don't have to hit a gym at all.

Movement and exercise should be a part of life, and you can do this at home, at work, or running errands on a weekend. You can do it alone or with family and friends or strangers.

Daily life is movement, and you can build more and more of it into everything you do. Set your intention on *walking*, finding ever-longer distances in your routine. Perhaps you'll pass a park you didn't know existed the next time you walk the long way. By adding a little time to your trip, you add great benefit. Perspiration releases toxins, your heart rate elevates, oxygen-rich blood circulates, your blood pressure drops, and you feel great, all from a brisk 10 minute walk after lunch. Or do a few yoga stretches at your desk between meetings. Leave free weights in the laundry room and do 25 reps each time you turn a load over. Cut the shrubs with manual hand shears, not electric. Everyday activities can help make you fit; it's cumulative and it all counts.

Many communities offer access to free gyms, indoors and out. Check out what your options are and don't hesitate to take full advantage of what your town or city has to offer. However, if you don't want to follow organized fitness, get creative. Mop the floors to a fierce beat. Play ball with neighborhood kids. Go online to YouTube and move along with a workout video. Cable networks sometimes offer a fitness channel where you can watch everything from yoga demonstrations to weight-lifting techniques. These tools are like having a personal trainer! Use them. Explore the apps on your Smartphone. Read the reviews. Most are inexpensive and some, surprisingly comprehensive. Find what works for you. You can never grow bored; there are just too many options!

Investing time into movement is as important a daily activity as brushing your teeth, sleeping, and getting good nutrition. If you aren't moving enough to quench the needs (and desires) of your mind-body physiology, you'll pay later.

If you don't move, you will fall prey to even more disease as you age. (Perhaps the time you did not spend exercising will now be spent in doctors' waiting rooms?) That does sound harsh, but why would you wait until any situation got that bad? Why not start moving and rewrite the end of your story? It too can be filled with vibrant life and health. Time, you see, passes much more quickly during exercise than it does from a hospital bed. Conquering the "time" problem in your head brings us to our next step, visualizing yourself as a fit person.

Visualize Yourself as Fit into Your Future

Use your visualization skills to project yourself into the future. What will you look like at 40, 50, 60, 70, 80, and beyond? In one scenario, you're climbing Mount Kilimanjaro at 67 or boogie-boarding with the grandkids at the beach. Look the other way and you are overweight, ill, and bedridden, a true elderly person long before your time. It's a simple as the answer to the question, where do you want to be? Visualizing yourself as a healthy person is a powerful tool in getting your head in the right place to move. That healthy person you see in your mind's eye is what you are working toward every single day of your life. Put your intentions on that person and send your vibration into the universe. Put your energy on that healthy human and start moving, every day. This is a huge gift of love and a better life for your-self. You, fit and healthy, is a sight we want to see.

Focus on the Astonishing Mind-Body Benefits

In this step, you've gained a lot of knowledge. You understand the huge benefits that movement offers your cardiovascular, immune and endocrine systems. You understand its deep positive effects on your mind and your body. On a large level, exercise enhances stamina and energy levels. It also helps you fight off disease and cellular deterioration as you age. It is, as they say, a fountain of youth.

To be specific, regular exercise improves your heart and blood vessels, guarding against heart attack and stroke. The musculoskeletal system is strengthened, building both muscle and bone. Respiration and perspiration detoxify the body from the chemicals in processed foods, household cleaners, beauty products, plastics, and air, ground, and water pollution. Regular exercise aids in the digestive process (digestion, absorption, and elimination of waste) and has been shown to cut colon cancer rates in half. Movement releases carbon dioxide and waste products from body tissues into the bloodstream and on to the filtering organs, where it is processed and eliminated by bowel movements, perspiration, and urination, a powerful detoxification. And, of course, working out controls weight and cellulite.

In fact, movement reduces overall cancer statistics and has been shown to have a huge impact on adult onset diabetes. The enhanced cardiovascular activity of exercise carries nutrients and oxygen to every cell, energizing and accessing peak perfor-mance in everyone who does it regularly. Mental clarity, flex-ibility and energy are always the result. That is why we do it:

Movement makes you feel really good and sharp and "on your game." Who doesn't want to feel like that? It's joyful.

Mood Enhancement to the Max

Ever come home at the end of a stressful day feeling anxious, tense, and reactive? Everything rubs you wrong? You need movement to counter negative feelings, obsessive thoughts, anger, anxiety, and other symptoms known as depression.

Physical movement is your best defense against cortisol, the stress hormone your body releases under threat that can also wreck you if left unchecked. Your brain has a "fight or flight" mechanism that kicks into drive when you feel threatened: It's instinctive. (Your ancestors once stayed alive based on their ability to sense an attack from the many forces that wanted to turn them into dinner.) Today, your threats have changed (bosses, bills, kids), but the reaction has not. Counteract cortisol by moving your body and releasing your feel-good hormones called endorphins. Unknot muscles where tension lives. Let your brain go blank. Now, you'll be on your way to a safe, natural treatment for negative thought and physical exhaustion. It also promotes good sleep, a key to neurological health and regeneration. Each night, your brain recharges itself, processing experiences into memory. As you dream, the "wires" in your brain are jumping in a dance mostly unknown to our waking selves, but essential.

Limitless potential lies inside our bodies. We have the ability to counter disease by activating what's inside us already. As the yogi sage Sahara said, "Here in the body are the sacred rivers: here are the sun and the moon, as well as all the pilgrimage places. . . . I have not encountered a temple as blissful . . .

Renowned integrative medicine pioneer, Dr. Andrew Weil, frequently prescribes aerobic exercise as a preventative measure and treatment for depression. He maintains that "aerobic exercise works, in part, through the release of endorphins, a class of endogenous antidepressants made in the brain. It both treats and prevents depression in susceptible individuals." Weil recommends 45 minutes of aerobic movement 5 days a week. "Any activity that raises your heart rate and gets you breathing fast will do. Walking is fine but do it fast enough or include some uphill time."

I love my early evening walks with my pooches, strolling at twilight and enjoying the sights of my neighborhood. I do it every day as a way to mark the end of work and the beginning of evening time when I focus on my family and myself.

For me, this movement is highly personal, but aspects may resonate with you. My evening walk reconnects me to the natural world—sunlight, grass, insects, birds, and the vibration of all living things. I am reminded of the vastness and complexities of all life. The magic and wonder I feel is a perfect transition back to my core being at the end of a long day. My nerves become quiet and my mind begins to still. I return to this same activity each day in all of its infinite varieties. As you can tell, these walks do a great deal for my spirit, and the pooches just love it!

If you can find an activity as personally satisfying to you as I find my early evening walk, odds are you will continue to do it. Think about what you love—walking, stretching, dancing—and engage in engineering activities just for you. If you want company, plenty of folks (and pets) will join your movement. Ask your partner, neighbor, colleagues, or a friend.

12

sacred love

Body is art, art is the sensual nature generated into the life of spirit.
—BETTINA VON ARNIM

Sexuality is our creative nature. Gaining an understanding of the importance of sexual energy as it relates to birthing beauty and wellness may be one of the most important things you can do for yourself. Terra incognita for some, the ocean of life for others, our sexuality is a subject that deserves much exploration. The multifaceted nature of sexuality plays an enormous role in our lives. It is one manifestation of energy—the libidinal type.

From Tantra to soy, self-love to dang gui, fantasies to Kegels, there are a wide variety of natural and organic approaches to enhancing our sexuality. Yet sexuality can be fraught with many misconceptions that stem from our upbringing and cultural influences. Our views on sexuality can be as different and diverse as our religious teachings, socioeconomic status, ethnic heritage, and education.

Interestingly, if someone lives life on a higher vibrational level, external constructs placed on sexual expression do not figure into the scenario. The human body is pure vibrating energy. As we access the higher vibrational aspects of our being, we become more connected with spirit. The more connected we are to spirit, the more apt we are to ignore—or at least overlook—external influences in our life. In short, we don't care what anyone says. At this more evolved point, free-flowing sexuality can fruitfully blossom, reseed itself, and continue to flourish throughout a lifetime.

Begin with Yourself

Reaching this higher vibrational level means that you are in a place where you have divine knowledge of and communication with self—or, more organically put, spirit. You should know that it all begins with the love, intimacy, and sensuality expressed first to yourself. When you know what gives you pleasure, you will more effectively communicate this special information outward.

Part of this remarkably nurturing higher plane is understanding the erotic beauty surrounding you at every moment. Look deeply to understand how this beauty affects and arouses you. Orgasmic energy surrounds and flows through you. Enjoyment of the erotic is about our love for beauty. In the caves of Lascaux, there is a famous painting of a hunter who has shot an arrow into a buffalo, and that hunter has an erection. Why do you think this is? He has prayed to his god to provide food and clothing for his tribe. That god has blessed him with these provisions. He has made a connection with the divine. The beautiful and mighty buffalo spirit will become one with the tribe through the food that they eat and the skins that they wear.

This is pretty heady stuff! And for this hunter, it is quite the turn-on. But it illustrates how we all experience varying forms of arousal and, yes, ecstasy as we watch life unfold. And again, as through our journey together here, exquisite mindfulness fruitfully brings this experience into our consciousness. Every one of you reading this has a personal interpretation of the erotic beauty that surrounds and arouses you. What we need to learn, however, is how to recognize, respect, and connect with this form of beauty.

As you learn about your own sexuality, you'll have more insights into the universal nature of this energy: It flows everywhere. Others might not express it exactly the same way you do, and that is exactly how it should be. Remember, we are talking about the sacred whole, and that means accepting and celebrating this energy in all its manifestations.

Sexuality as Universal Energy

Healing traditions from the earliest times to the present include sexuality as a sacred expression of the divine. Out of the womb of creation comes our sexuality. It is the dance of life that balances, renews, regenerates, and reproduces. One divine creative energy flows through all things, giving life. This creation is God's love flowing through and between everything that is.

Becoming a loving person is an integral part of living organically. This includes loving Mother Earth, your neighbors, your family, your significant other, and yourself. What's more, love in the organic sense reaches beyond the traditional meaning of intimacy. It includes compassion, empathy, enchantment, commitment, and many other emotions.

One important facet of love is our sexuality and the ways we express it. Blockages in our sexual energy impede our free-flowing ability to express ourselves and realize our desires. To discover and release your sexuality, you want to begin by looking inward and reflecting on who you are, why you're here, and what it is that truly makes you happy. Make clear your desires, visualize them, and give them a voice. Positively affirm your desired outcome. Fantasize to fuel the erotic imagination. As the Caribbean-American writer Audre Lorde wrote, "There are many kinds of power. . . . The erotic is a resource within each of us that lies in a deeply female and spiritual plane, firmly rooted in the power of our unexpressed or unrecognized feelings." Through mindfulness and exploration, you too will learn about those feelings.

To understand your sexuality, realize that it is born from a healthy sacral chakra, part of our chakra or energy system. Yes, you are born this way. Located in the area of the navel, lower abdomen, sexual organs, and lower back, our sacral chakra has a great impact on our creativity, sexuality, relationships, empathy, pleasure, emotion, and intimacy. A healthy sacral chakra enhances our ability to go with the flow, be filled with grace and acceptance, and allow us to enjoy our lives and achievements. The hips, lower back, sexual/reproductive organs, kidneys, bladder, stomach, large intestine, pelvis, appendix, and bodily fluids are all associated with this chakra. If you feel that you have imbalances in any of these areas, consider further exploration to balance the sacral chakra. Affirm that you allow your creativity, your sexuality, and your emotions to flow though you in a healthy, life-affirming way.

To further understand your sexuality and sensuality, know that it begins in your mind and your heart, not your genitals. Sociocultural and religious upbringing can tarnish or repress our views of sexuality by fusing the concept with the actual act of sex. Sexuality may also be distorted through media and advertising exploitation, which sends mixed messages loaded with sexual innuendos and overtones. And we can't forget the fear connected to sexuality as we associate sexuality with the act of sex and that act with potential trauma: sexually transmitted disease, unwanted pregnancy, sexual abuse, rape, human trafficking for sex, and problems defining or defending our sexual identity. Now for good measure, let's throw in anxiety, as some of us struggle with our ability to have children, our ability to perform, PMS, menopause, and impotence. Clearly, the topic of our sexuality can bring up many stressful issues.

These issues are all the more reason to do some soul-searching and open the communication channels within yourself and between you and your loved ones. (Furthermore, call upon your holistic health care professional where appropriate to assist in any challenges and help with healing.) Only then can we receive and give love in the organic sense, loving all those who are dear to us with compassion, empathy, enchantment, and commitment. Then we are free to add the actual act of sex and all its accompanying passion where it's appropriate to the relationship.

Sacred Love

When we make love from a higher level of consciousness, we experience the sacredness, the divinity, and the exquisite pleasure of union with God. Whether it is a matter of loving yourself or loving your beloved, lovemaking ideally includes a keen awareness of every sensation in your body and learning how to modulate the way in which you physically respond to these sensations. Controlling your response to these energies in your mind-body physiology allows for a heightening of the entire experience—the merging oneness with divinity.

Whether you enjoy Tantra or remain with your own practices, it is paramount to have conscious, compassionate loving sex as often as your desires dictate. It is an important pillar of our well-being. The physical pleasures and benefits go without saying, and the benefits in deepening a relationship with your partner can greatly affect your overall health and wellness. Visualize having regular loving intimacy as an important part of your day-to-day life. If you are experiencing loss of desire for intimacy—and this is not a physiological problem but one of simply feeling fatigued and overextended in other areas of your life—you now know that you can turn that situation around. Extreme self-care is the answer. You have the will to do this. Positively affirm that you will simplify your life to be able to include regular enjoyment and expression of your sensuality, sexuality, and intimacy.

Healing traditions from the earliest times to the present day include sexual energy as a sacred expression of the divine. Out of the womb of creation comes our sexuality. This divine energy flows through all things, creating and giving life.

Becoming a loving person is an integral part of living organically. This includes loving the earth, your neighbors, your

Self-Love

Self-love can be the wellspring from which we come to know and enjoy ourselves deeply and intimately. One of the reasons that 20 percent of all women rarely experience or never have an orgasm is that they never have been adequately aroused. Man or woman, by taking responsibility for your own arousal, you have the ability to turn this around. Self-love allows you to find out what really turns you on and makes you feel good. When you become aware in this way, you are able to enjoy a more dynamic experience if and when you are in a relationship with someone special. Like many things in life, it may take a little practice, so practice.

significant other, and yourself. What's more, love in the organic sense reaches beyond the traditional meaning of intimacy. Compassion, enchantment, sensuality, commitment, joy, and many other emotions come into play.

Naturally, an important facet of love *is* our sexuality—the libidinal type—and the way we express it. However, a number of saboteurs can take us away from our most loving self. "Feeling the love" takes commitment on our part. It's easy in today's stressful and time-starved world to let sexual satisfaction fall by the wayside. Some of you reading this may want to renew this wonderful relationship with your sensual, sexual self.

Since the body's central organ of sexual response is the brain, "organic" brain food can include blissful aromas, luscious tastes,

enlivening colors, mesmerizing music, warm baths, sensual massage, fragrant flowers, candlelight, the feel of silk on bare skin,
feathers, reading erotica, skinny-dipping, moonlight—you get the
idea! In addition, should a researcher have your brain waves on
a monitor during stimulation of your sexual organs, your entire
brain will light up with activity. Yup, the brain loves it too.

In Tantra yoga, the pursuit of sexual pleasure has long been
a form of sacrament, considered as essential to nurturing life as
food and water. Perhaps on your erotic journey you'll consult the
ultimate manual on Tantra lovemaking, the *Kama Sutra*—written
by Vatsyayana 2,000 years ago, about the same time as the Bible's
Book of Revelation. Deepak Chopra has done a lovely updated version of this sacred ancient text.

A mélange of worship, meditation, ritual, and mysticism, this
tradition teaches that sacred love leads to a direct experience with
God. To the yogic practitioner, Tantric worship transforms orgi-
astic energy into a spiritual force that delivers the worshipper to
the divine. Whether loving yourself or your beloved, lovemaking
includes exquisite consciousness and modulation of every sensation felt in concert with the breath. In other words, the true
pleasure of sex doesn't come from orgasm but lies in recognizing,
receiving, and satisfying our lover.

Tantric yoga assigns a central role to the senses in the quest for holy
enlightenment. Loving touch, ritual bathing, sacred soundscapes,
ecstatic dance, sensuous fabrics, herbs, aromatic oils, and body paint,
along with edibles such as dried and fresh fruits, healthy nuts, cham-
pagne, and chocolates (chocolate-dipped strawberries and dried apri-
cots, yum!), are kept close at hand to titillate the tongue and refresh

the senses. I encourage further study of the *Kama Sutra*, a comprehensive prescription for pleasurable living that incorporates aspects of mythology and astrology. And of course, there are the sixty-four enlightening "art of sex" passages. A big reason for the *Kama Sutra*'s lasting fame and centuries of devoted practitioners is that it equally emphasizes our spiritual desires and sexual satisfaction, considering our human need to feel appreciated and emotionally connected.

And by the way, many high-profile spas offer workshops on sacred loving. Of note is the eco-organic Miraval Tucson resort and spa in Catalina, Arizona. The program was featured on *Oprah*; that's how mainstream this subject has become.

There's also a magnificent book written by one of the most sensual and green wise women on the planet, Diana De Luca. It's called *Botanica Erotica: Arousing Body, Mind, and Spirit.* This playful and provocative guide to the aphrodisiac foods, herbs, and behaviors that arouse us will provide the ingredients for a lifelong exploration of sensual pleasure. You'll find recipes in the book that you may want to make (organic ingredients, of course!), such as candied edible flowers, chocolate spiced butter, Tantric trail mix, Damiana (*Turnera aphrodisiaca*) cordial, and much more.

So many marvelous companies offer organic lotions, oils, lubricants, and "love" toys that I will leave it to your own resourcefulness to research them on the Internet. However, I would be remiss if I didn't mention my friend Wendy Strgar's company Good Clean Love (www.goodcleanlove.com). I so appreciate reading Wendy's blog "Making Love Sustainable," and her organic "love" products are simply divine! As you pursue your own erotic nature, log on to read Wendy.

13

clearing and filling the body: an earthly vessel for spirit

The circling rivers, the breath, and breathing it in and out,
The beauty of the wrist, and thence of the hips, and thence downward toward the knees,
The thin red jellies within you, or within me—the bones, and the marrow in the bones,
The exquisite realization of health;
O I say, these are not the parts and poems of the Body only, but of the Soul . . .
—WALT WHITMAN

So much of what we have talked about entails cleaning the mind and spirit and filling it up again with goodness and vibrant life. We all get depleted and forget our joy, but a life committed to filling the soul again is a life we all want to live.

Let's get started by really cleaning out our vessel.

Life Is Perpetual Renewal: Detox, Rejuvenate, Renew the Soul's Vessel

Your intention here is to lighten your body's toxic load. Toxins come from outside—think air pollution, too many plastics,

177

chemicals in body care products and packaging, food additives and packaging, alcohol, cigarettes, prescription drugs, cleaning chemicals, and even fertilizers—and assault the body from birth to the end of one's days.

The body itself produces toxins as by-products of certain functions (metabolic waste, digestive or hormonal by-products, free radicals, along with toxic thoughts and emotions that create real changes in the body's chemistry). Along with all the other toxins that arrive via your lungs (in the air), your skin (all the products you use), and what you ingest with foods, internal toxins should be purged too. In a perfect world, all would be engineered for human wellness and health, but alas, this world is not perfect. So make time to detox. It could save your life.

As toxins build, you might reach your "body load," the tipping point where too many harmful substances weaken the immune system and create mental fogginess, extreme fatigue, skin problems, body aches, neurological ailments, endocrine disorders, heart disease, and even cancer.

The lymphatic, respiratory, urinary, and gastrointestinal systems and the skin all function to detox your body, but because your loads are increasing every day, your vessel needs your help.

Detox it and build it back up. That's an overarching mantra for your journey into loving the vessel for your soul, your spirit's lair. That's the cycle of all the earth: spring, summer, fall, and winter. Try not to wander too far afield of nature's way. That's how we stay in harmony with it all.

Celebrate Life through Dance or Let Your Spirit Fill Your Body

I've shown you how to clean the vessel, and now I'm going to show you how to fill it up my way. If you did not guess this already, I love dance. I can find no better fusion—for me—of body movement and soulful expression. I enjoy dance as one of the meditation in motion activities I love along with yoga and walking. I also teach it in my wellness sessions and even conduct ecstatic dance with large conference audiences.

The Incredible Benefits

Did you know that dancing makes you smarter? A major twenty-one-year study funded by the National Institute on Aging and undertaken by the Albert Einstein College of Medicine tracked senior citizens and demonstrated how stimulating the mind by dancing increases cognitive acuity at all ages and can ward off dementia, much as physical exercise keeps the body fit.

As an aside, there is no blood barrier between the rest of the body and the brain. Therefore, the good things you do for one enhance the other and vice versa. Conversely, every insult to the body reverberates in the brain. You are a whole organism and should view yourself in that fashion. Everything you do—and do not do—affects everything about you.

Now, back to the study that wanted to see if any physical or cognitive recreational activities influence mental acuity. They discovered that some activities had a significant beneficial effect. Other activities had virtually none.

continues on page 184

The Big Clean

How to Detox

From a practical standpoint, you may need help getting started on your detox. There are many ways to do it, and you can make it your priority several times a year or integrate it daily into your self-care and wellness routines.

Some of these ideas you've already read about, and others may be new.

1. Slow down and connect with your inner peace. This allows you to tune in to your thoughts and actions and truly be present with yourself and others.

2. Smile and be kind. If you're warm-hearted when greeting others, they'll often respond in the same way. This encourages healing energy to flow between you and them. It enhances all your interactions and keeps toxic thoughts away.

3. Think positively. Minimize disturbing influences and release toxic thoughts as soon as you have them. Remember Dr. Candace Pert's statement that each negative thought becomes a molecule in the body.

4. Toxic thoughts can create some of the same chemical changes in the body as pesticides. That's why a positive mind-set is critical for long-term health. If you don't think it, you don't release destructive chemicals.

5. Learn to forgive. Even when justified, anger and resentment are poisonous. Anger and jealously drag

you deeper into your dark feeling and bind you to the object you feel has wronged you. You must let these feelings go, and yes, it can be hard.

6. Enjoy every facet of nature as often as you can. It provides tremendous life-force-enhancing nourishment for the body, mind, and soul. The Japanese call this an earth bath, and here we talk of earthing. In both systems, the object is to be in a heavily oxygenated space, in tune with nature and away from human-made sound. For earthing, stand in your bare feet on grass for twenty minutes and you'll keep your blood thin and flowing.

7. If you are a smoker, quit. It is a well-documented toxic activity. Prescription medications are available as well as a wide variety of over-the-counter smoking cessation aids. While you're at it, avoid secondhand smoke both while you quit and then forever. Your doctor can assist you with this as well.

8. Reduce exposure to pollution. Diffuse purifying essential oils into your environment. Invest in an air purifier. Heavy humidity and smog alerts should be taken seriously. Do not take on strenuous activity in heavily compromised air. Keep your lungs healthy by breathing clean air.

9. Eat plenty of fiber: more whole grains, beans, nuts, and brightly colored cruciferous vegetables (cabbage, broccoli, brussels sprouts, avocado, kale, asparagus, spinach, and green beans). Fiber (whole grains, cauliflower, lentils, black beans, pears, pistachio nuts,

raspberries, hummus, Greek yogurt) will bind with and remove toxic compounds in the colon and pull them out while increasing regularity. Eat from these lists as many times as possible during the day.

10. Eat plenty of antioxidant-rich organic vegetables and fruits, especially those which are deep colored. Reach for reds, yellows, and greens. Antioxidants help neutralize free radicals: harmful reactive molecules that can set the stage for chronic and acute disease.

11. Consider juicing as you reach your daily vegetable target with ease. At the same time, it's your hidden shortcut for detoxification, genuine healing, and optimal weight. This has become a science and a flavorful craft, and you'll find recipes to keep you whirling for a long time.

12. Drink eight to ten 8-ounce glasses of purified or filtered water daily. Hydration is a key component in detox and all aspects of health. Add the juice of a lemon for further detoxification benefits. Do not use lemon if you have issues with heartburn.

13. Exercise at least thirty minutes every day. It not only will reduce stress but will increase and improve circulation, which will enhance the body's natural detoxification process. Don't forget about those feel-good endorphins that are produced! You'll be surprised have much you move in the course of a day now that you are putting your intention to it. You do not even have to join a gym; just hit the stairs!

14. Meticulously care for your skin to flush toxins. One-third of metabolic waste is excreted through the skin. A daily cleansing and hydration ritual is important. Remove eye makeup with cotton and an organic makeup remover. Use a gentle face cleanser and rinse your face at least five times a day in fresh water. Take the time.

15. Get regular massages; better yet, give yourself a daily massage. Use an organic plant oil to massage your body. Do this before you shower in the morning. It'll optimize the skin's barrier function, lymph system flow (moves toxins out of the system), blood circulation, and lubricating joint fluids. It also will unknot those muscles and release a flood of feel-good chemicals into the bloodstream.

16. Go to bed early and rise early to optimize the regenerative effects of sound slumber. Our bodies— and spirits—love to move in rhythm to the sun.*

*Portions of this list first appeared in Mary Beth Janssen, "15 Ways to Limit Your Toxic Intake," *Organic Spa Magazine*, June 18, 2016.

They studied cognitive activities such as reading books, writing for pleasure, doing crossword puzzles, playing cards, and playing musical instruments. They studied physical activities such as playing tennis or golf, swimming, bicycling, dancing, walking for exercise, and doing housework.

One of the surprises in the study was that most of the physical activities appeared to offer very limited, if any, protection against dementia. There can be cardiovascular benefits, of course, but the focus of this study was the mind. There was one important exception: the only physical activity they tested that offered protection against dementia was frequent dancing.

Reading decreased the risk of dementia by 35 percent, bicycling and swimming had no effect on the brain, doing crossword puzzles at least four days a week decreased the risk of dementia a whopping 47 percent, golf had no effect, and dancing frequently lowered the risk of cognitive impairment by 76 percent! Besides the fact that I just love it, can you see now *why* I love it?

We were born to dance! It has been shown to do the following:

- Reduce stress and depression

- Increase energy and serotonin levels

- Improve flexibility, balance, strength, and endurance

- Strengthen bones and boost cardiovascular health

- Increase mental capacity by exercising the cognitive processes

- Stimulate dynamic and rapid-fire decision making, creating new neural pathways

What's not to love about dance, knowing you'll reap these incredible wellness benefits for the mind-body physiology? But wait; there's more.

Everybody Dance

Dance comes naturally to all of us. Look at babies! As soon as they are on their feet, babies are dancing. They don't know it, of course, but the way their limbs move freely is truly the first dance we all do.

We feel good when we dance. Our bodies move to a rhythm and our minds become free. The heart gets a great workout, pumping oxygenated blood everywhere. Endorphins, our feel-good hormone, flow. As we dance and become more in tune to the music and our bodies, the mind disengages. It lets go, letting us just be.

Dance-therapy organizations abound. That's because dance is intensely therapeutic. It serves as a healing tool for personal expression and overall emotional wellness. Folks with physical disabilities, addiction issues, sexual-abuse histories, eating disorders, and other concerns all benefit by expression through dance.

Think beyond *Dancing with the Stars* and the waltz, foxtrot, rumba and salsa. I've attended ecstatic, or trance, dancing, which is the most primordial of all dancing movement. Like all dancing, it frees the mind and connects with us to our inner spirit. Shamans, the Sufi whirling dervishes, and other shamans and indigenous peoples have trance-danced for thousands of years, and this healing technique has regained popularity.

Ecstatic Dance

I'd like to share ecstatic or trance dance with you right now; it is one of my favorite total awareness workouts. The most important advice I can give you is to trust the process. Let it unfold organically. All you have to do is truly be there. You may experience yourself as spaceless and timeless.

You don't need a great deal of physical room since the dance happens largely within. However, if you have more room, you can become more expansive in your movements and get the juices flowing more quickly. It's all good.

- Turn on a musical selection that allows you to tune in to the rhythm and move freely. Begin by standing with your feet parallel to your shoulders and let your body and mind relax.

- You may want to close your eyes so that your eyes see only the vast inner landscape of your consciousness.

- Become aware of your breathing. Inhale and exhale deeply, filling your lungs entirely. Do this for a few minutes; it will awaken the energizer within.

- Relax and allow your body to move to the rhythm. Soon you will feel the life-force energy moving through your body. At this point, you as the dancer will disappear and you will become the dance. You've awakened spirit. Focus completely on your body and your movement. It's in this place that you can experience profound emotions, a letting go, and a peaceful connection to your own immortality.

This entire process can go up to thirty minutes or more. When I'm sweating—or "sweating my prayers," as Gabrielle Roth, goddess of the dance and founder of the 5Rhythms method, is known to say—I know that I've arrived. It really is pure ecstasy. I highly encourage you to visit Gabrielle's website (www.5rhythms.com) and YouTube channel to study her method and integrate it along with all the other techniques you are learning. It's the best medicine for whatever ails you.

When the music ends, take several minutes to be still. How was your experience? This can be the ultimate meditation in motion because dance is one of the most playful ways to connect with spirit.

Anyone can dance. There's no right or wrong way to do it; it's just natural, organic movement. Our bodies love to move; they're meant to move. Just like the Sufi whirling dervishes, you swirl, chant, and channel thought and emotion as you dance your way to ecstasy. Turn on your favorite music, close your eyes, and let spirit move you. Let your inner dancer come out and play. I dare you!

Fill and Empty, Fill and Empty

Methods to purge toxins from the body are pretty much the same, but there are infinite roads to filling the spirit. We talked about a few of the ways to fill the vessel—meditation, visualization, yoga, breathwork, physical movement, time in nature, reading, daydreaming, and more—and you have so much to explore on your own. I am excited for you and your beginner's mind!

We have touched on many of these ideas repeatedly in this book, but this is your new normal, the way of life you choose, and as you move forward, you can't hear this enough. Life is organic and ever changing. Toxins—from stress, pesticides, human-made chemicals, aggravating loud noise, lack of space, and multitasking—have taken a toll on our way of life. Therefore, a part of your job—what you owe yourself—is to keep your system as clean as you can so that it can function as optimally as when the Creator made it. Consider a consistent plan to clean your "vessel of spirit," your body's insides and outsides, as you move forward with love, health, and self-care.

14

come back to your senses

Remember only the beautiful things that you have felt. And seen, and experienced. If your five senses behold only the good, then your mind will be a garden of blossoming soul qualities.

—PARAMAHANSA YOGANANDA

We metabolize life through our senses. If we can learn to breathe in life through all our senses, it will change the way we experience our world. Everything becomes more vivid—tastes, sights, sounds—and we see brighter colors, have stronger memories, and become more receptive to others. Our senses are the sacred gateways to our consciousness. Our outer environment melds with our inner environment to profoundly affect our mind-body physiology. If you are feeling discomfort, uneasiness, or imbalance of any kind, you can use your five senses to create great healing and pacifying influences for your nervous system as well as the energy field that surrounds you. Your five senses will serve you in the same remarkable fashion as you explore the expansiveness of your mind, body, spirit, and environment through the many activities discussed in this book. Your senses are the way you take in information in regard to *everything*.

Yet sometimes we forget how to use our greatest tools and gifts. It doesn't need to be complex. I suggest you take a moment, slow down, and look within. Deep down inside, you know the difference between healthful and harmful as they pertain to your body. Tap into the nourishing wisdom that is inherent within you. You know what is best for you; you "sense" or feel it. Exercise. Nutrition and hydration. Sleep. Stress relief. They are integral to the optimal functioning of your faculties. These practices keep your immune system humming along in top form and keep you sensually tuned in to your inner and outer worlds. It is so easy today to disregard and neglect the five senses through cumulative mindless actions and the oblivion of habit. I urge you to witness what you do and surround yourself with a world that is touching, easy on the eye, tasty, music to the ears, and heavenly fragrant. When you do, you're nurturing the life force within you and surrounding you.

Although none of us can control our environment all day long—think about that stress-filled commute or that hot, crowded waiting room—we can mitigate the effects. As you pass through anything challenging, merely use the meditation, visualization, and breathwork you've learned in this book. Lessen the aggravation with a mini-meditation and get yourself into a positive pleasing place as soon as you can. Don't forget to breathe.

In *The New Culture of Desire* by Melinda Davis (at the helm of The Next Group in Manhattan, strategist behind The Human Desire Project,

The Big Six

The six primary senses that have great healing power for us, others, and our environment are as follows:

* Healing sounds include the sounds of nature, chanting, toning, and mantras, along with music, drumming, and the sound of silence.

* Therapeutic touch can detoxify tissues, enhance relaxation, and stimulate the immune system.

* Sense of taste is nature's way of informing us of her nutritious gifts.

* Aroma can be used to relax, stimulate, and balance the mind-body physiology. Studies have shown time and time again that smell is the strongest evoker of memory.

* The sense of sight allows us to take in nurturing sights and colors that enhance attention, balance our energy system, and enliven creativity. Color is associated with feeling as well.

* The "sixth sense," or our inner voice, is engaged through contemplative techniques. This allows for positive thoughts, healthy emotions, and nurturing beliefs.

Fortune 100 "hired gun visionary"), the author talks about our culture's need for the "state of O," or "optimal state of mind." We seek "peace of mind" and pleasurable healing, and this begins with our ability to engage in the practice of sensuality. Naturally, the wonders of tuning in sensually have tremendous benefits. We need to feel this deep connection, peace, joy, and exhilaration in our bones. We seek ecstatic life.

Let's take a journey through the senses and see how we may up our sensuality quotient (SQ).

Our Sense of Sound—All Is Rhythm

Gabrielle Roth said, "Rhythm is our universal tongue. It's the language of the soul."

Think of sound as the nutrition of vibration. Breathing, chanting, toning, drumming, mantras, the sounds of nature, and any form of music can all be profoundly healing. They nourish the nervous system, create greater brain wave coherence (harmony), and release healing chemicals and hormones into the bloodstream. The sound waves that we take in trigger nerve cells that send electrical energy to the brain. The nervous system translates these impulses as pleasant—serving to relax or invigorate the body—or unpleasant—causing the body to feel stress. Pleasant sounds enhance immune system function, produce endorphins, and bathe us in joy-inducing neurotransmitters. Vibrating sounds create resonating energy fields. These energies can alter our breath, pulse, blood pressure, muscle tension, and skin temperature, among other physical changes. Since we are also vibrating energy, this makes total sense—the sense of sound, that is!

All individuals have their own response to sound, depending on the situation they're in. Driving rhythm can stimulate and inspire us, whereas sedative, ambient sounds can be very soothing. This includes chanting, drumming, and any form of repetition. We can alter our mood depending on the surrounding sound in any given moment. This experience will be different for everyone. We can perceive sound as healing and evocative or toxic. Intrusive, irritating sounds are linked to high blood pressure, lower productivity, zapped mental and creative energy, and higher serum cholesterol levels. Studies also show that in the presence of continuous noise, people are less caring, communicative, and reflective and more likely to feel helpless and powerless. Think about the "soundscape" that you travel through every day from the time you get up in the morning until the time you go to bed at night. Don't simply ignore or passively adjust to noise pollution. Eradicate it.

We all know songs that bring us joy, power our workouts as well as our workplace productivity, and help us snooze or unwind. Compile an easy-listening section on your iPod for those times when stress has the upper hand. Or simply start watching your breath or go for a walk in nature. Pay attention to the sounds that surround you. In your beauty and wellness environment, ratchet down the decibels.

Blaring music takes us away from our focus and work. Use electrical products that have the lowest possible decibel rating. Consider decorating with soft surfaces that absorb noise. Install

continues on page 196

What We Can Learn from the
Salon/Spa Environment: A Sensory Experience

In my day job, I do a great deal of work with holistic salons and spas. We can take ideas and implement them in our lives and homes to enhance our development as those places do for their clients. The environment is vibrant, energizing, and devoid of as many environmental stressors as possible. Only natural, organic materials are used in products. It has never been more important to cherish our health and our energy. As we care for ourselves, we are more able to care for others, especially those we love:

* Bring yourself fully into your environment. Be present.

* Create a glowing, comfortable space with comfortable seating, plump pillows—whatever is most pleasing to you.

* Deliver a healthy and serene setting that is good for your creativity.

* Serve only delicious, nutritious food and beverages. Serve yourself in real glasses and on real plates. No throw-away items, please.

* Provide wonderful sights from a fresh and clean station to flowers and all manner of beautiful colors.

* Full-spectrum lighting simulates natural daylight. Colors are truer, and fatigue is lessened. No fluorescent bulbs.

* Offer calming sounds, including music. Cut the noise pollution—modulate sound levels.

* Provide the most healing aromas. Ventilation ensures an ongoing supply of fresh air.

* Engage all the senses with nurturing toxin-free products, preferably organic.

* You're earth-friendly. Recycle and reduce consumption. The environment is built from as many natural, sustainable products as possible.

* Water should be purified. Invest in a water purifier for your faucet or a water cooler. Drink the cleanest water available to you, eight glasses a day. Add a slice of lemon or thin slices of cucumber to enhance taste and refreshment.

* In your home, use as many natural fabrics—cotton, silk, linen—as possible. Not only do these fabrics feel good to the skin, they are less likely to irritate it. Soften laundry with a cup of vinegar (it doesn't smell when the clothes are dry) and some essential oils. You can also add a scent to your clothes by filling a spray bottle ¾ full with water and adding essential oil until it smells good to you. Spray it on your clothes as they come out of the dryer.

baffles and double-glazed windows. And do, do, do consider modulating the musical vibe, selections, and decibel levels to please you and those around you. You may consider designating one day or night a week for "techno-ambient grooves," another for "operetta delights," and yet another for the jazz greats. Explore music from all genres and cultures, a project that would take many lifetimes to even make a dent in all that sound!

Our Sense of Touch

"I was so touched by what you said" and "We've lost touch with each other" are statements from our daily conversations. Truly, touch serves as a metaphor for a deep and soulful connection with others. We may indeed be touched on a variety of levels, with the most healing and visceral being the laying on of hands.

The skin is the body's largest organ, with as many as 5 million touch receptors, 3,000 in a fingertip alone. With loving attention—whether massaging our own skin or touching another's—there is tremendous healing power in our hands. If you haven't experienced the wonders of this practice, what are you waiting for?

Stroking the skin releases a pharmacy of natural feel-good chemicals into the bloodstream:

- Natural growth hormones

- Natural antidepressants

- Natural tranquilizers

- Natural pain relievers

- Immunomodulators
  (boost the immune system)

- Vasodilators
  (open the blood vessels)

Use a holistic and preferably organic body oil or lotion to give yourself a self-massage. You may do this at any time of the day; however, doing it in the morning before showering has tremendous benefits for centering you for the day ahead. Make this part of your meditative practice to commune with the self. Starting at the scalp, gently massage yourself from head to toe. Where appropriate, use upward and outward movements. Be fully present with yourself as you perform this amazing ritual. Have the intention to send loving energy to yourself. Any tension that you feel will melt away as you languish in this mood-enhancing practice. At the very least, massage your scalp, hands, and feet at any point during the day or before going to bed. I keep an organic lotion at my bedside to indulge in this ritual every night. I promise you will experience sound slumber and maybe even a sweet dream or two!

It's critical to be aware of the power of our hands and the energy that they transfer. We can experience this on a very subtle level by using simple grounding or centering rituals and when receiving a haircut, facial, manicure or pedicure, or full-body massage. You may choose to give your scalp, neck, shoulder, or hand a massage as part of this grounding ritual. Sink deeply into relaxation. Ultimately, you will feel a sense of release, calm, and safety. Turn off all the noisemakers and be totally present to yourself as you do this. Remember, as we give, so we receive, and that applies to you when you are giving to yourself.

Our Sense of Taste—Nourishing Wisdom

You might be surprised by this statement because you do this three times a day most days and may not even think about it. And that's the trouble. So I say eating is a sacred act. Why? Because we become the food we eat. It fuels our body, our mind, our emotions, and our soul. With that in mind, do you still want to eat mindlessly, not tasting and not thriving? Reflect on your eating habits. Slow down. Choose foods that speak to the senses and feed the body. Don't burden your individual remarkable heavenly chemistry with "fake" foods. Processed foods—items engineered with chemicals to last on the grocery shelf—also leave those chemicals behind in the body. They are at best empty calories and at worst harmful to your health. Consider what you eat in a typical day at work as well as a day off to assess how and why you eat. Make the changes. Again, the right foods, true natural nutrition, will transform your life.

In addition:

- Take in as many whole, natural, organic foods and eliminate as many processed and refined foods as possible. In this way, you dramatically lessen your exposure to chemical toxins.

- Include a combination of high-quality protein, complex carbohydrates, and good fat at every snack or meal.

- Enjoy whole grains, legumes, nuts and seeds, and fruits and vegetables (in abundance). All these are high-fiber, nutrient-packed foods.

- Stay hydrated over the course of the day. Drink at least eight glasses of purified water. Sip a little aqua regularly throughout the day to keep the metabolic processes humming along.

- Avoid trans fats: anything that says "partially hydrogenated oils."

- Bolster your energy levels by eliminating or reducing your intake of caffeine, white flour products, and simple concentrated sugars. You will control blood sugar levels and lessen the likelihood of insulin resistance, storage of fat, and high cortisol levels (read high stress load and adrenal exhaustion).

- Lessen your intake of ice cold beverages (particularly with meals) and foods to avoid squelching the digestive fires.

- Eat in a quiet settled environment; do not eat when emotionally overwrought.

- Eat only when hungry. Listen to your appetite.

- Eat at a comfortable pace. Slow down. Stay conscious of the process. Don't overeat. Leave a portion of your stomach empty to aid digestion.

- Sit quietly for a few moments after eating and focus on the sensations in your body. Ask yourself, "Does everything feel divine?" Listen to your body and witness how it reacts to your food choices. Do you feel satisfied? Alert?

- After eating, go for a short walk if possible. It will optimize digestion.

- Do take a high-quality multivitamin with antioxidants and drink brightly colored fruit and vegetable juices without added sugar. The more color in a plant's bounty, the more phytochemicals to clean out the free radicals in your cells.

- Visit your dentist regularly. The Centers for Disease Control (CDC) reports that one in three of us have tooth decay. Consider a tongue scraper to remove any coating from the tongue first thing in the morning (this is a by-product of the detoxification that takes place overnight).

- Floss and brush after every meal and keep natural breath mints or drops on hand.

Our Sense of Smell

Helen Keller said it best: "Smell is a potent wizard that transports us across thousands of miles and all the years you have lived."

We all know aroma's healing powers. The scent of lavender relaxes, rosemary invigorates, a passing woman's perfume reminds you of your mother. Smell also intimately connects us with memory and emotion. I might steal a whiff of Brut cologne at the local drugstore to vicariously relive my youth and remember my dating years with my now-husband James. Freshly mown grass, baby powder, my rosebush out back, a fragrant Cabernet Sauvignon, freshly ground coffee, the air after a thunderstorm—all these are evocative fragrances. I'm sure you can think of a few of your own.

The nose has millions of scent receptor cells that bind with aroma molecules to send electrical impulses into the brain's limbic system, the seat of our emotions, memories, intuition, and sexual response. The limbic system also affects the nervous, hormone, and immune systems.

In aromatherapy, pure essential oils can be used to create a sense of balance to relax and to stimulate. Aromatherapy can boost confidence, help destress, detoxify, sooth aching muscles, enhance metabolic and other bodily functions, and purify our environment.

We also use pure essential oils to purify, moisturize, tone, balance, rejuvenate, and provide astringency for the skin, hair, and nails. Because everyone's experiences and body chemistry are unique, we all have a highly individual reaction to aroma.

Here are a few general guidelines for using aroma to care for oneself and/or alter one's environment. An essential oil air diffuser is an economical and effective way to fill your space with aroma. Choose the oils on the basis of your needs that day. Here's a partial list of essential oils and the symptoms each one relieves:

Emotional? Excitable? Anxious?

Use calming oils that are floral, fruity, warm, and sweet: rose, lavender, geranium, orange, basil, clove, vanilla. You may find them useful for relieving restlessness, anxiety, cramps, backache, heart palpitations, and insomnia.

Fiery? Jealous? Overly Intense?

Soothe, clarify, and ease the mind with oils that are cooling, sweet, bitter, and astringent: sandalwood, mint, rose, jasmine, chamomile, lily, iris, honeysuckle. They are useful to relieve anger, impatience, jealousy, ulcers, inflammatory bowel disease, and skin conditions.

Sluggish? Susceptible to Depression? Complacent?

Lighten up and enliven with pungent, spicy, stimulating oils: rosemary, lemongrass, eucalyptus, cedar, sage, musk, juniper, clove, marjoram, peppermint. You may find them helpful for their energizing qualities. They can increase motivation and are useful in releasing attachment to and retention of food, fluid, fat, relationships, and unhealthy emotions.

Please consider that just as there are powerfully evocative and pleasing fragrances, there are also toxic smells. Environmental pollution in our personal and work environments requires attention. Try to wean yourself from products with strong chemical smells, have adequate air filtration systems in place, and if possible surround yourself with cleansing green plants. Get as much plastic out of your immediate space as possible, especially in the form of bottles and eating utensils. Reach for glass, wood, porcelain, and stone.

Keep your olfactory apparatus in tip-top shape. Consider a neti pot (found at your local drugstore, online, or at your local yoga studio) for daily nasal washing. The results can be astonishing for alleviating allergies and sinusitis.

Great smell starts with you. Personal hygiene and scent should be a part of every one of your days. People will be drawn—or will withdraw—on the basis of smell. It is that powerful and operates on a level beyond most people's awareness. Smell the way you feel happiest, and ideally the world will like it too. Hygiene matters each and every day for optimal well-being. Smell good for yourself and others.

Our Sense of Sight

Not to get too metaphysical on you, but our sense of sight may refer to that which we take in through our visual apparatus as well as

Essential Oil Delivery Systems

You may use aroma/essential oils in the following ways:

* Use neat (direct) as in lavender or tea tree oil placed directly on the skin. Please note that most essential oils may not be used in this fashion. Work with a qualified aromatherapist to determine any contraindications and safe use.

* Use a diffuser.

* Use in a spray to mist the environment.

* Add to organic plant oil/lotion for massages or facials (or certainly one of the many fine preblended oils/lotions available).

* Light a high-quality aromatherapy candle (organic soy, lead-free wick).

* Add to manicure or pedicure water.

* Use in hydrotherapy and bathing to scent the water and hydrate the skin.

* Potentize a treatment, shampoo, or conditioning service by adding oils to the liquid before you use it.

* Make sure that you are using 100 percent pure essential oils, preferably organic, with no synthetic fillers, suspending agents, or added mineral oil.

* Consider furthering your education to learn more about some of the over 700 essential oils in existence. There are precautions and contraindications that any reputable training program will address.

that which we see in the mind's eye. We literally think in pictures. Visions become memories, both good and bad, that we visit and revisit all our lives. Sight brings us so much in life.

See the beauty in everyone. As we search for beauty and wellness, we can see the beauty in each person and bring it gloriously outward. When we do this, we are sharing our inner sight: our ability to visualize creatively. Resist the temptation to judge on the basis of external appearances. We have the power to see a person's individual beauty and indeed to help the entire world see it.

The same is true of your beauty. Focus on what you most love about yourself whether it's your eyes, your legs, or the way you move. Whatever pleases you about yourself, focus on that and celebrate it. Part of learning to see beauty is understanding that is *always* in the eye of the beholder; in this case, that's you.

See the Light

Our eyes gather light and shoot it via neurons off to the brain, which makes sense of what we see. We then define, categorize, and label it. We take about 70 percent of all sensory information in through the eyes, where a large number of sense receptors are clustered. Did you know that more than 25 percent of the nutrients we absorb from food go to nourish the visual system? Simply amazing and an excellent motivation for eating as healthily as possible. Who among us wouldn't want to keep our vision clear for as long as possible? (For the record, foods heavy with vitamins C and E, zinc, lutein, zeaxanthin, and omega-3 fatty acids are all great for the eyes.)

Visualize beauty:

- Practice creative visualization on a regular basis to "see" yourself in a beautiful place that engenders a sense of peace and joy. Inundate your senses in this place: the colors, textures, aromas, sights, and sounds. You may also use your visualization skills coupled with positive affirmations to see yourself manifesting that which you desire.

- Reduce exposure to disturbing imagery. Tragedy, violence, and mayhem kick the body's stress response into high gear. Doctor Andrew Weil recommends that on occasion we go on a news fast. Good advice! The saying "You can't unsee that" is unfortunately all too true.

- Check your environment. Do you see and thus feel beauty? Is it cluttered and sloppy or fresh and vibrant, ripe for your creativity? Remember, it's all vibrating energy. Clean it up, make it safe and beautiful, and love your space as you learn to give yourself kindness and love.

- Whether in your home or in your work environment, consider green plants, fresh flowers, and the colors that you surround yourself with. Think of textures and softness. It might be as simple as a delicate bud vase at your workstation with the always present fresh flower. The Volkswagen Bug is certainly on to something with the built-in dashboard bud vase!

Color Your World

Color is electromagnetic energy. It has great power and can have a profound effect on the mind–body physiology. At home and at work, color can influence energy flow and activity throughout the space.

Chromotherapy is used to change bodily vibrations through colored light. Reds, oranges, and yellows are stimulating, giving off energy and strength. Warm and/or muted colors can calm restlessness or anxiety (gold, muted orange or yellow, deep purple, indigo). Purple induces lightness of being and enhances intuition. Greens and blues are cooling, cleansing, and balancing.

In chakra balancing work, a different color relates to and balances each one of the energy centers. Whether meditating on the color, breathing the color in, wearing the color, eating the color, or surrounding ourselves with the color, we begin to change the vibration within the chakra that we're working on, with the potential for great healing to take place. For example, if we feel that our communication skills could be improved, we surround ourselves with blue, the color of the chakra of the throat, home of our expression and communication. Close your eyes, breathe deeply, and visualize blue. You may also wear blue clothing and eat blue foods such as blueberries and Concord grapes. You will be harmonizing the vibration of the light spectrum that is the blue in your body.

Heavy stuff, huh? Some of you are already working with these concepts; others are hearing this for the first time. If it is of interest to you, there is plenty of further education on the subject. Become a seeker. Find it and learn! All are a part of traveling the path toward wholeness in mind, body, and spirit.

The Chakras/Energy Centers

* **Root/base of the spine**—home of our basic survival instinct—the color red.

* **Pelvic area/reproductive organs**—the seat of creative/biological energy—the color orange.

* **Navel/solar plexus**—where we manifest our intentions and desires—the color yellow.

* **Heart**—home of compassion and love—the color green.

* **Throat**—center of expression/communication—the color blue.

* **Brow/third eye**—the center of our insight or inner voice where we envision fulfillment—the color indigo.

* **Crown/top of the head**—where our individual and universal aspects connect and create awareness of our spiritual nature—the color purple.

The Sixth Sense: Making the Divine Connection

We've visited this subject time and again in this chapter. This is where we are able to connect with our inner vision and voice through contemplative and centering techniques, whether through prayer, meditation, visualization, positive affirmations, or regular connection with nature. We become more mindful of what our inner voice is trying to tell us as we quiet down the overactive mind, or monkey mind, as they say in the East.

The feminist poet May Sarton said, "Loneliness is the poverty of spirit; solitude is the richness of spirit." Some of us may need to practice becoming quiet, enjoying solitude, and listening to the broad and universal aspect of ourselves that can be found within. This is where pure consciousness resides, and it is the field of infinite possibilities.

Lessons Learned on the Road to Sensual Healing

One of the most important lessons that I've learned in trying to open up to the sensuous is to simply sit back, breathe, and be here now in blessed idleness. Yes, meditation is powerful for connecting us to our source. But we do this so that we, in all our sensuousness, may profoundly turn outward from our bodies, not turn inward toward our minds. It is a matter of being able to pay exquisite attention to everything that's swirling around us and being able to home in on the beauty.

Let me leave you with this:

"If you atrophy one sense you also atrophy all the others, a sensuous and physical connection with nature, with art, with food, with other human beings."

—Anais Nin, *Diaries*, **Vol. 2**

acknowledgments

I want to express my heartfelt gratitude to my literary agent and soul sister, Lisa Hagan. You walked with me side by side through one of the most difficult periods in my life, which happened to coincide with the creation of this book. Without your continued support, enthusiasm, and inspired guidance, this book would not have come to fruition. Your loving-kindness and compassion are boundless. Om.

I am incredibly appreciative of Beth Wareham, a supremely creative talent, whose virtuoso efforts helped to bring this project to the finish line.

Very special thanks also go out to my brilliant and heart-centered editor, Kate Zimmermann, along with the stellar team at Sterling for creating such a stunningly beautiful book. I feel very blessed to have had this book produced by this exceptional and very synergistic publisher.

index

Healthy boundaries (*cont.*)
  and daily mindfulness practice, 142
  defining needs, 142
  importance in self-care, 139, 140
  and meditation, 143
  setting, 140, 141
Heart
  opening the, 40, 41
  brain, 37
  as chakra/energy center, 37, 207
Heraclitus, 97
Hydration, 182
Hypertension, 104
Hypothalamic-pituitary-adrenal axis, 57

J

Immunomodulators
  in natural healing system, 15
  role when skin is stroked, 196
Inner voice, healing power of, 191
Institute of HeartMath, 39
Intention
  advantages of, 93–96, 97
  going with the flow, 97, 98
  and mindfulness, 93
  sharing, 98

J

Jesus, 13
Jordan Grafman, 47, 48
Journal, combating stress with a, 65, 66

K

Kabat-Zinn, Jon, 82, 83
Kahn, Dmatt, 129
Kama Sutra, 175
Karma
  and conditioning of soul, 21
  cleansing our, 33, 34
  definition of, 32
  law of, 36

Keller, Helen, 200
Kindness, 48
Kornfield, Jack, 46
Kumbhaka, 124

L

Lamott, Danne, 139
Lao Tzu, 89
Lavender oil, 203
Law of Karma, 36
Lipton, Bruce, 15, 54
Lorde, Audre, 170
Love-based karma, 32
Loving-kindness meditation, 43–45
Lymphatic system, 178

M

Mantra
  and brain, 103
  and meditation, 108
  practicing a, 111
  phrase, 80, 95
  using a, 109
  vibrational quality of a, 110
Massage
  as beautifying ritual, 28
  and endorphins, 16
  and essential oils, 203
  as means of detoxifying body, 183
  as means of diffusing stress, 66
  and meditation, 113
  in natural healing system, 10
  as organic brain food, 173, 174
  as sensory modulation technique, 61
  self-, 79, 197
Meditation
  concentrative, 107, 108, 110
  doing it correctly, 112, 113, 114
  establishing a practice, 102
  and healing breath, 108
  and healthy boundaries, 143

Top of the head as chakra/energy center,
207
Touch, therapeutic power of, 191, 196
197
Trance dance. *See* Ecstatic dance.
Transcendental Meditation and mantra,
109
Tulku, Tarthang, 1
Twain, Mark, 157, 158

U

Unity consciousness, 25
Urinary system, 178

V

Vasodilators, 196
Vedas, 23
Vegetables, 182
Vinyasa yoga, 158
Vision, creating a, 26
Visualization skills
and beautiful objects, 205
and physical activity, 162, 163
Von Arnim, Bettina, 167

W

Waits, Tom, 130
Walking
and effect on body, 149
and sense of ease, 147

War veterans and meditation, 103
Weight-bearing activity, 159
Weil, Dr. Andrew, 117, 118, 205
Well-being, optimal, 2, 3
Whitman, Walk, 177
Wilde, Oscar, 2
Witnessing the present moment, 75,
76–78, 79
World Health Organization and statistics
on depression, 154

Y

Yeshe, Thubten, 31
Yoga
asanas, 10
and awakening, 79
and breath retention, 125, 126
and breathwork, 123, 125
healing benefits of, 103
centering yourself with, 111
and emphasis on posture, 120
and healing movement, 143
and "Namaste," 43
and meditation, 25, 106, 107
and mindfulness, 71
and natural systems of healing, 9
and pranayama, 124, 189
Tantra, 174
and veterans of war, 103
vinyasa yoga, 158